At the Supermarket
在超市

请把单词和对应的图连上线吧!

money •

shelves •

shopping cart •

cashier •

shopping bag •

At the Shopping Centre
在购物中心

单词对应哪个图呢？请你把对应的图圈出来。

 salesman

 watch

 hamburger

 menu

In the Farm
在农场

这是什么动物？下面的单词与图对应吗？对应的，请画勾 ✓；不对应，请画叉 ×。

goat

donkey

pig

sheep

cow

3～8岁

WORDS for ESL LEARNERS

情景英语4000词

2 场景会话 1000词

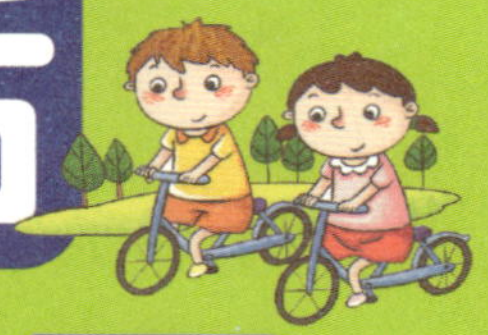

练习册

ACTIVITY BOOK

北京大学出版社
PEKING UNIVERSITY PRESS

Happy Birthday
生日快乐

这两个单词你认识吗？请你为蛋糕和礼物涂上漂亮的颜色吧！

birthday cake

present

It's Sunny Today
今天阳光灿烂

图上的单词对吗？对的，请画勾 ✓；不对的，请画叉 ✗。

barbecue

tent

soil

water

grass

Pet Show
宠物展览会

这些宠物多可爱啊！请你把与图对应的单词圈出来。

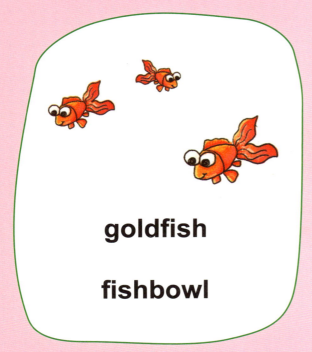

goldfish

fishbowl

butterfly

tortoise

rabbit

bird

parrot

carrot

New Year and School Concert
新年和学校音乐会

下面的图对应哪个单词？请你连连线。

At the Zoo
在动物园

请你为它们涂上颜色吧，再把单词读一读。

lion

giraffe

zebra

At the Zoo
在动物园

图上有哪些动物？请在对应的单词后面画勾 ✓。

| pigeon ○ | swan ○ | hen ○ |
| panda ○ | elephant ○ | snake ○ |

goose ◯   chick ◯   flamingo ◯

crocodile ◯   parrot ◯   hedgehog ◯

At the Beach
在海滩

图对应哪个单词呢？请你把正确的单词涂成红色。

At the Circus
在马戏团

这些单词对应哪个图？请把序号写在对应的框里。

① tent　② cannon　③ unicycle　④ clown

In the Playground
在游乐场

下面的单词与图对应吗？对应的，请画勾；不对应，请画叉。

At the Library and Cinema
在图书馆和电影院

这些图对应哪个单词？请把单词的序号写到对应的框里。

① **a pile of books** ② **cinema**

③ **screen** ④ **librarian**

At the Airport
在飞机场

这两种飞机用英语怎么说？请你为它们涂上颜色吧！

airplane

helicopter

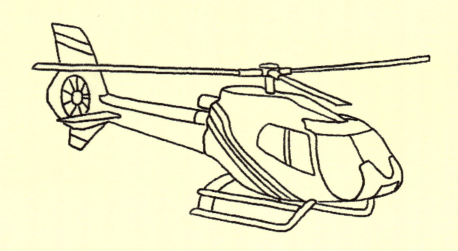

At the Train Station
在火车站

下面的图对应哪个单词，请你连连线。

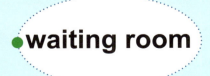

17

At the Subway
在地铁

下面的方框里，有几个"passenger"？请把它们涂成红色。

passenger

p	a	s	s	e	n	g	e	r	p
s	c	r	c	r	e	p	a	s	s
p	a	s	s	e	n	g	e	r	p
a	c	s	a	s	r	s	a	e	r
e	w	c	o	a	o	p	s	s	e
n	p	a	s	s	e	n	g	e	r

Let's Go for a Ride
我们去兜风

图对应哪个单词呢？请你把对应的单词涂成红色。

gas station   gas pump

wheel

traffic lights

cyclist

road sign

trash can   tire

19

At the Hospital
在医院

哪些单词与下面的图对应？请你把单词框涂上颜色。

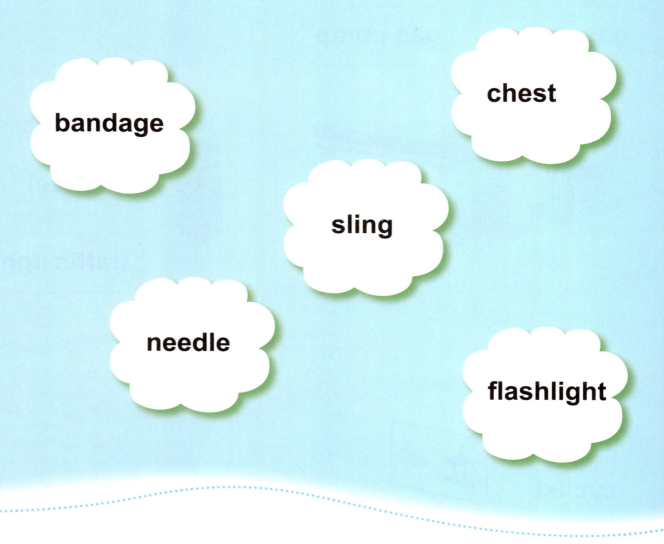

- bandage
- chest
- sling
- needle
- flashlight

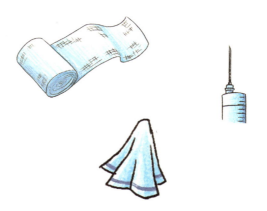

eye chart

doctor

handkerchief

nurse

inject

drill

At the Barbershop
在理发店

读一读这些单词，再与对应的图连上线吧！

mirror   **hairdresser**

shampoo   **hairdryer**

Father Is a Builder

爸爸是建筑工人

请读出下面的单词,并把与它对应的图圈出来。

crane

workman

ladder

Uncle Is a Fireman
叔叔是消防队员

图对应哪个单词呢？请你把对应的单词涂成红色。

fire engine **hydrant**

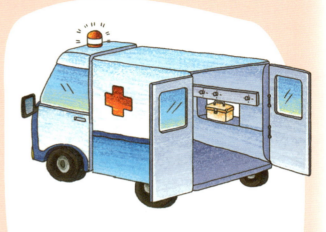

smoke **ambulance**

mask **horn**

axe **helmet**

Police Officers Help David
警察帮助大卫

请你圈出与"警察"相关的词,并读一读。

policeman

sand

police station

policewoman

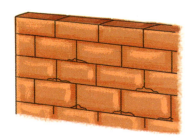

bricks

Cleaning Courtyard
清扫院子

请读出这四个单词，再画上对应的图。

broom

fallen leaves

gloves

trash can

Going to the Post Office
去邮局

请把对应的单词和图连上线吧！

package

carry

envelope

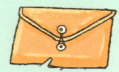

postman

post office

Let's Go for a Boat Ride
我们乘游艇

下面的图对应哪个单词呢？请你把对应的单词涂成红色。

It's Time to Get Up
该起床了

单词对应哪个图？请把序号写在图旁边。

① quilt　　② alarm clock　　③ wardrobe
　　　　④ bed　　　⑤ pillow

Get Dressed
穿衣服

根据提示，圈出对应的单词。

穿在身上的有哪些？

shirt

sweater

comb

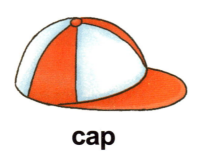
cap

T-shirt

Breakfast
早餐

下面哪些是能吃的，请画勾 ✓；哪些不能吃，请画叉 ×。

Going to School
上学啦

请把对应的单词和图连上线吧！

wait　　　　run

cycle　　　walk

In the Classroom
在教室

请为单词画上图，或看图选出正确的单词涂上红色。

blackboard	
glue	
blue	
paper	
scissors	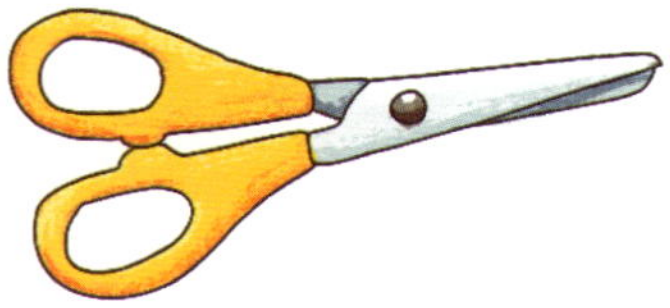
sisters	

Playtime
游戏时间

下面的单词对应哪个图？请你把图圈出来吧！

jump

ride

swing

In the Kitchen
在厨房

这是什么电器？请在下面的方格里圈出这个单词，共有5处哦！

refrigerator

r	c	r	c	f	e	p	a	s	s	o	r
p	e	s	s	e	n	g	e	r	p	r	e
r	e	f	r	i	g	e	r	a	t	o	r
e	w	c	r	a	o	p	s	s	e	e	a
n	p	a	s	i	e	n	g	e	r	o	f
r	e	f	r	i	g	e	r	a	t	o	r
p	a	s	s	e	n	e	e	r	p	f	n
a	c	s	a	s	r	s	r	e	r	e	a
r	e	f	r	i	g	e	r	a	t	o	r
n	p	a	s	s	e	n	g	e	t	r	e
r	e	f	r	i	g	e	r	a	t	o	r
n	p	a	s	s	e	n	g	e	r	a	r

Dinner Time
晚餐时间

下面的图对应哪个单词呢？请你把对应的单词涂成红色。

In the Bathroom
在浴室

请把对应的单词和图连上线吧!

washcloth　　mirror　　bath tub

shower

bubble　　　　　　　tap

Bedtime
睡觉了

单词对应哪个图？请把序号写在图旁边。

① kiss   ② toy   ③ sleep   ④ comic

动手动脑趣味多
英语越学越快乐

使用说明

① 学完一个主题做一个练习，以达到复习巩固的目的。
② 家长为孩子念题，引导孩子自主完成。
③ 孩子练习时家长给予鼓励，孩子完成后要及时评价、表扬。

WORDS for ESL LEARNERS
情景英语4000词

① 基础分类 1000词

练习册
ACTIVITY BOOK

3～8岁

北京大学出版社
PEKING UNIVERSITY PRESS

Family
家庭

他们是谁？请把单词和对应的图连上线吧！

Body
身体

这些单词对应身体的哪一部分？请把序号写在对应的框里。

1 eye   2 nose   3 neck   4 arm
5 ear   6 mouth   7 teeth   8 hand

Things We Wear
穿戴衣物

请你为它们涂上漂亮的颜色,再大声地把单词读出来吧!

coat

dress

In the House
在屋子里

单词对应哪个图呢？请你把图圈出来。

sofa

television

telephone

soap

In the Kitchen
在厨房里

请你划掉不属于厨房里的东西,再把"在厨房里"的单词读一读。

pot

watch

stove

glasses

bowl

plate

chalk

In the Classroom
在教室里

这些单词是什么意思？请把它们画出来吧！

pencil

ruler

eraser

book

读一读这两个单词，再把滑梯和风筝涂上喜欢的颜色吧！

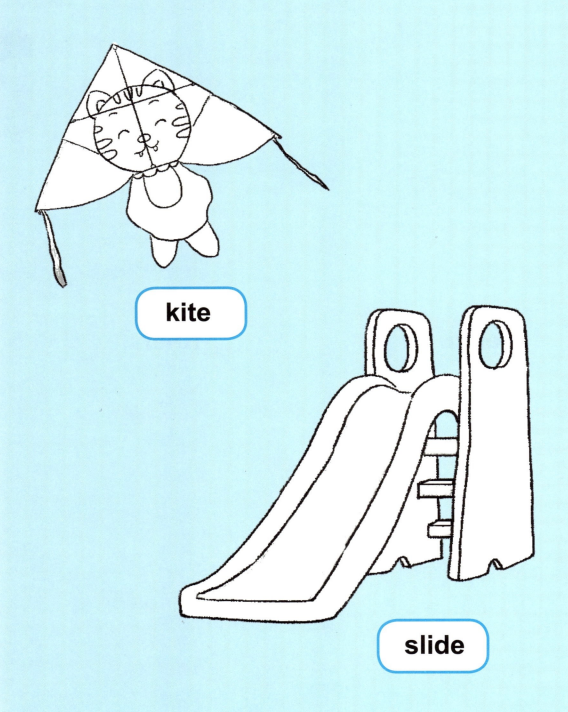

kite

slide

下面的图画对应哪个单词？请你圈出来。

tablet

thermometer

syringe

stretcher

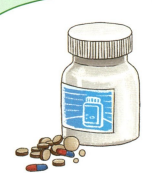

medicine

bandage

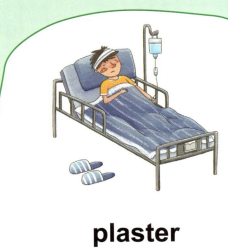

plaster

patient

In the Garden
在花园里

图与旁边的单词对应吗？对应的，请打勾 ✓；不对应的，请打叉 ×。

Farm Animals
农场动物

多可爱的小动物啊，请你为它们涂上颜色吧，再把单词读一读。

dog

cat

cock

下面的动物对应哪个单词,请你连连线。

Aquatic Animals
水生动物

你能读出这两个单词吗？再把图的另一半画出来吧。

crab

starfish

鸟类

"小鸟"和"鹦鹉"的英语怎么说？请圈出正确的那一个。

pigeon　　　**bird**　　　**swan**

parrot　　　**seagull**　　　**eagle**

Insects
昆虫

下面哪些是昆虫？请你圈出来，再大声读出它的单词。

ant

pigeon

fly

bee

robin

cricket

Flowers and Fruits
花和水果

下面的方框里,你发现几个"rose"?请把它们涂成红色。

rose

r	o	s	e	r	e
e	o	s	s	e	o
s	e	r	o	s	e
o	r	s	o	r	o
e	r	o	s	e	s
r	o	s	o	s	r

请读出这四个单词,再画上对应的水果。

apple

peach

pear

orange

16

读一读这些单词，再与对应的图片连上线吧！

pumpkin

potato

bean

onion

cucumber

carrot

请在食品旁边涂上红色，在饮品旁边涂上蓝色，再把单词读一读。

cake

milk

tea

bread

pizza

fruit juice

Musical Instruments
乐器

这是什么乐器？请圈出正确的单词。

guitar   piano   drum   violin   harp   cello

请把对应的单词和图连上线吧!

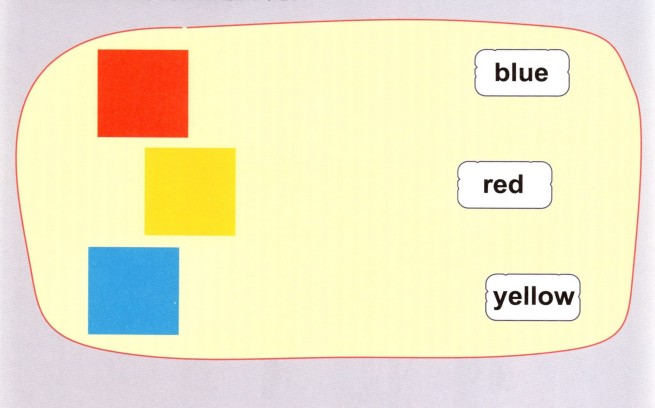

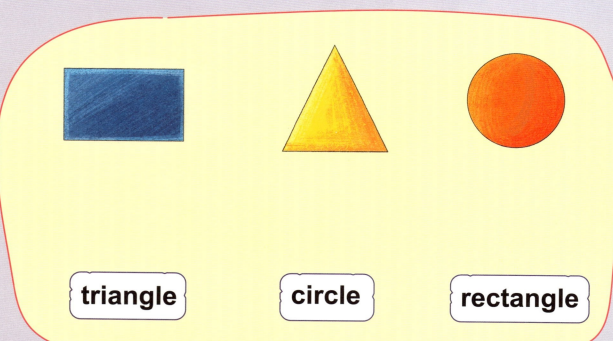

Numbers
数字

请你用英语数一数下面有几个礼物？再把它们涂上漂亮的颜色。

Buildings and Places
建筑物及场所

请读出下面这些单词，并把与它对应的图圈出来。

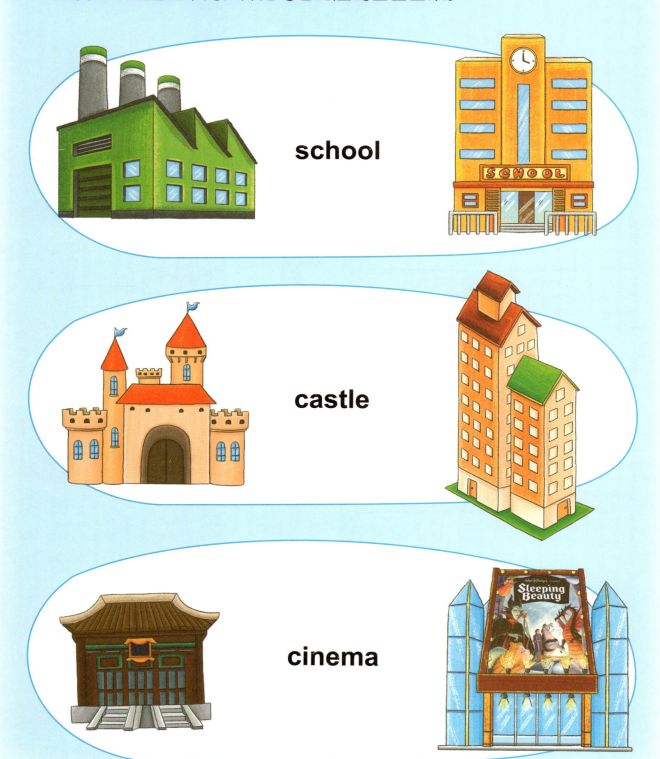

school

castle

cinema

下面的方框里，你发现几个"car"？请把它们涂成红色。

car

c	a	r	c	r	e
c	h	c	s	b	r
a	c	s	a	s	r
o	w	c	a	r	o
r	a	c	r	d	r
r	o	s	c	a	r

这些小朋友在做什么动作？请把他们和对应的单词连上线吧！

你知道下面这两组单词的意思吗？请把它们的序号写在图旁边。

1 on   **2** under

1 before   **2** after

Describing Words
形容词

请读出下面的单词,并在它对应的图旁边画勾 ✓。

small

cold

Machines and Tools
机器和工具

是谁这么粗心，把工具的名称贴错了。请你将图与正确的标签连上线吧！

Jobs
职业

你知道这些职业用英语怎么说吗？请把对应的单词涂成红色。

writer

firefighter

tailor

scientist

artist

actor

王子和公主的英语怎么说？请为他们涂上颜色吧！

单词对应哪个图？请你把图圈出来。

trip

picnic

Weather and Season
天气和季节

图表示哪个季节？请把单词和对应的图连上线吧！

autumn   summer   winter   spring

Nature
自然

下面的单词是什么意思？请为它们画上对应的图画吧！

sun

moon

star

rainbow

请为下面的气球涂上颜色。你还喜欢哪些玩具？用英语说一说。

balloon

这几个表示心情的单词用得对吗？对的，在圆圈里画勾 ✓；错的，在圆圈里画叉 ×。

Times of the Day
一日内的时间

图表示什么时间？请你把正确的单词圈出来。

morning　　　　**noon**

evening　　　　**night**

这是星期几？在这一天，你想做什么呢？请画出来吧。

Sports and Games
体育项目及竞赛

请在体育项目旁边画勾 ✓，再读一读这个单词。

tennis

roll

football

basketball

volleyball

sew

请把与图对应的单词圈出来吧!

universe  satellite

orbit  Mars

meteor  planet

People of the world
世界各国人民

读一读这些单词，再与对应的图片连上线吧！

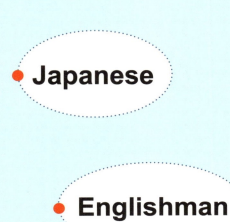
Japanese

Englishman

Korean

American

Chinese

Russian

动手动脑趣味多
英语越学越快乐

使用说明

① 学完一个主题做一个练习，以达到复习巩固的目的。

② 家长为孩子念题，引导孩子自主完成。

③ 孩子练习时家长给予鼓励，孩子完成后要及时评价、表扬。

步骤3：在趣味性学习中，逐步建立起属于小朋友自己的节奏

《情景英语4000词》提供一套三个阶段的学习模式。这种学习模式从感官（S）开始，过渡到语言（L），最终上升为思维（T）：S → L → T（下称 SLT 模式）。

S 阶段：

创造环境，鼓励小朋友主动识别图片，观察彼此之间的差别，实现最为准确的认识，并能说出图片的汉语名称。教小朋友单词，家长可以教，点读笔等也可以教。每个人的学习能力都不同，家长要有正确的评估和认知。对于孩子在图片、汉语和英语词汇之间的转化和关联上所表现出来熟练程度，家长需要格外注意，甚至在某些情况下应该留有记录。一个英语单词学习上所投入的时长，可以反映出英语习得能力的强弱。一般而言，时长与习得能力成反比。在学习初始阶段，家长有必要充分尊重小朋友的习得能力。如果超越习得能力而无休止地提高学习强度，恐怕只能拔苗助长，劳而无功。

L/T 初级阶段：

熟练掌握一个英语单词之后，可以适当提高学习强度。一方面，可以加入一些英语的基本句型，例如，"This / That / It is ..."，"There is a(n)"，"I see / find a(n)..."，"The (A)... is next / on the right / on the left to the (a)"，等等。这些基本句型以存在判断、感官判断和方位判断等为主，易于小朋友理解接受。另一方面，处于单词熟练掌握阶段的小朋友可以开始接触一些简单的思维训练，将个别对象归类为集合对象，这种最为基本的思维模式是主要的教授内容。例如，"Rabbit / Tiger / Cat / Dog is an animal"，"To wash, to clap, to kiss and to catch are things we do"，"Chalks, dictionaries, books and crayons are in the classroom"，如此等等。以上所给例句可谓最为简单的归纳判断，但是同时也是思维训练的开始和语言学习的基础。

L/T 熟练阶段：

老师或者家长可以尝试性地将演绎的思维模式渗透给小朋友，将上一阶段的学习模式翻转过来，集合对象成为聚焦的主体。例如，"For animal I know rabbit, tiger, cat and dog"，"The things we do can be to wash, to clap, to kiss and to catch"，"In the classroom, there are chalks, dictionaries, books and crayons"，等等。

整个 SLT 模式可以概括为下表：

阶段	步骤	认知内容	学习内容	家长注意事项
感官	1	图片	识别	鼓励、参与
语言	2	汉语词汇	在图片与汉语之间建立关联	保证对应准确
语言	3	英语单词	在汉语与英语之间建立关联；在图片与英语之间建立关联	体验、观察，甚至记录学习状况，根据个别单词学习时间长度大概确定习得能力
思维	4.1	英语语句	将英语单词纳入语句	主动引导，在丰富例句的同时鼓励尝试输出
思维	4.2	归纳	将个别对象归类为集合对象	注意例句的合理性和难度
思维	5	演绎	从集合对象中推演出个别对象	不做强求，顺其自然

《情景英语4000词》是英语学习的起点和基础，祝广大少儿英语学习者可以通过从感官到语言再到思维的过渡，最终实现英语的习得。

如果小朋友觉得学英文单词是一种有趣的游戏呢？

《情景英语 4000 词》3-8 岁孩子家长使用指南

 王威 北京大学英语博士，大连外国语大学副教授，硕士研究生导师。

英文单词学习痛点：单词应该怎么学？背单词太枯燥，单词量不够英语又很难提高。

推荐方案：有体系，有趣味，分类分场景的单词学习方案，实现让孩子"无痛"掌握单词，打好英文学习和提高的基础。

步骤1：选一套有趣的单词书

激发求知欲

从小朋友最熟悉的事物入手，把以前熟悉的名称转成英语，比如，"天空"变成了"sky"，"书"变成了"books"，"春天"变成了"spring"，让他们感受到陌生、变化与意外，激发求知欲。

克服不适感，增强可操作性

用新颖、好玩的方式，让有了好奇心的小朋友，恨不得立刻把所有原来知道的东西都转换一遍，在游戏中掌握知识。

从单词入手

英语单词，是英语语言之砖石，是英语思维之基石。掌握基础单词，在语言和思维之间搭建关联，既避开了语法和句法陷阱，又避免了一上来就对话的尴尬，将思维还原为语言，再将语言表现为感官，符合儿童认知发展规律。

《情景英语 4000 词》

包括<u>基础分类</u>、<u>场景会话</u>、<u>常用字典</u>和<u>常用动词</u> 4 个分册，各有一千余词，图文并茂、中英双语、纯正美语发音、配有练习和答案。可点读、下载 MP4 音频、扫码听音频和跟读测评。

小朋友可以看图，从形象开始，再听音，再知义，在英语和汉语之间实现关联，构建起食物、交通工具、心情以及位置等英语式思维内容，逐步实现语言学习→语言思维建立→语言应用的闭环。

步骤2：用一套有趣的学习方法，在有趣中消除对抗，变成自觉

❶ 亲子共读

所有的愿望与态度，都可以寓含在陪伴中。家长的态度，家长的方法，家长的情感，都可以通过亲子共读得到实现。学习的节奏，可以根据情景和效果进行调节、变换。

❷ 点读

点读笔的发明，让外教式的陪伴得以实现——哪里不会点哪里。图、词、句，都可以实现点读。

❸ 跟读、测评

要想学得跟母语一样标准，就是要反复模仿。模仿能力因人而异，但反复练习、自我纠正，必不可少。跟读之后，马上进行测评，可以反复进行，直到自己满意，让小朋友感觉到自己的进步，建立自信心。

❹ 学习，练习，复习，形成闭环

《情景英语 4000 词》一共四本书，并且配以四本练习书。练习书的题目类型多达十几种，充满挑战性和趣味性。

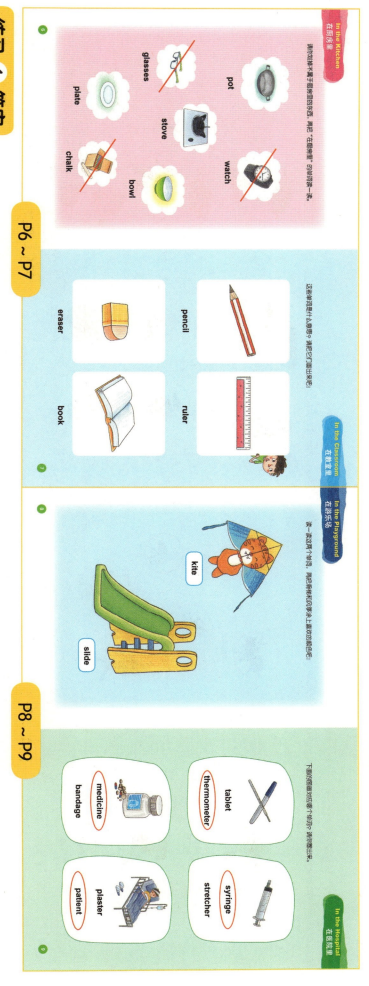
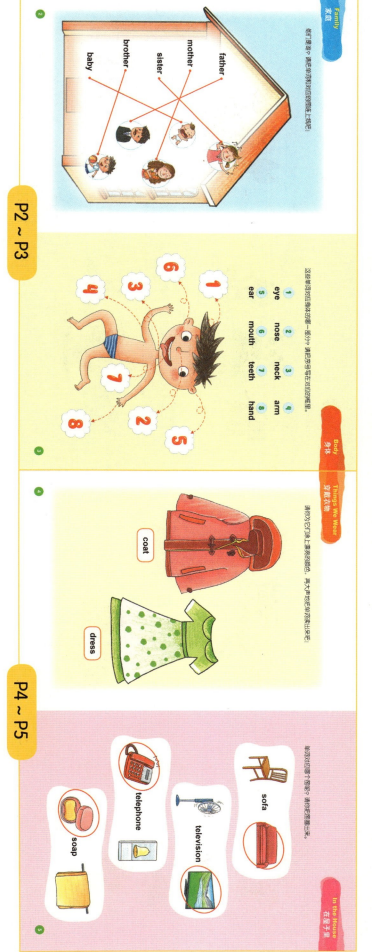

练习 1 答案

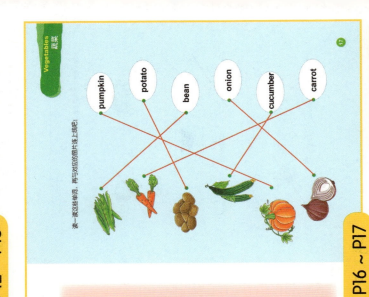

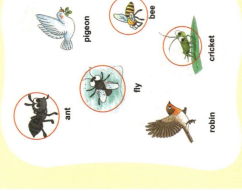
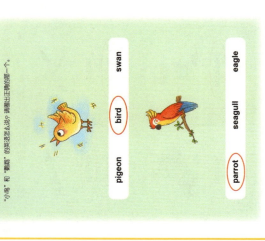
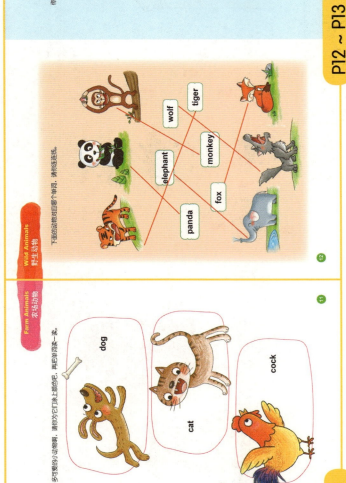
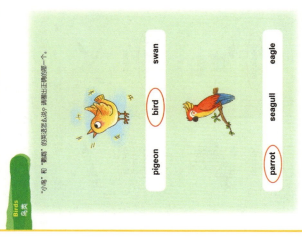

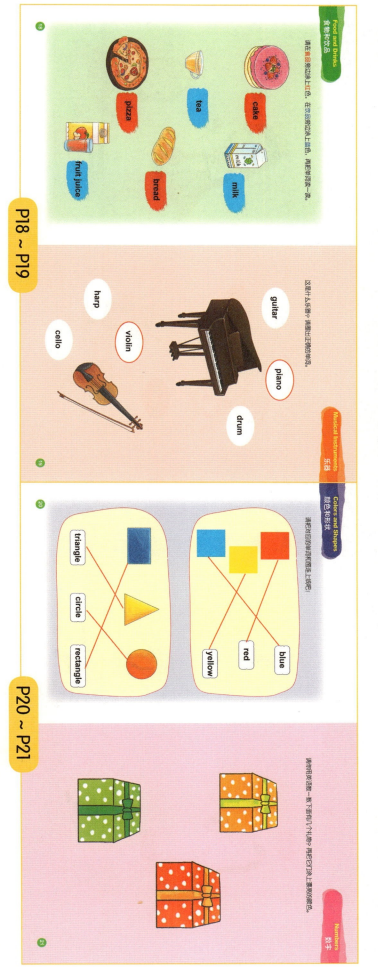
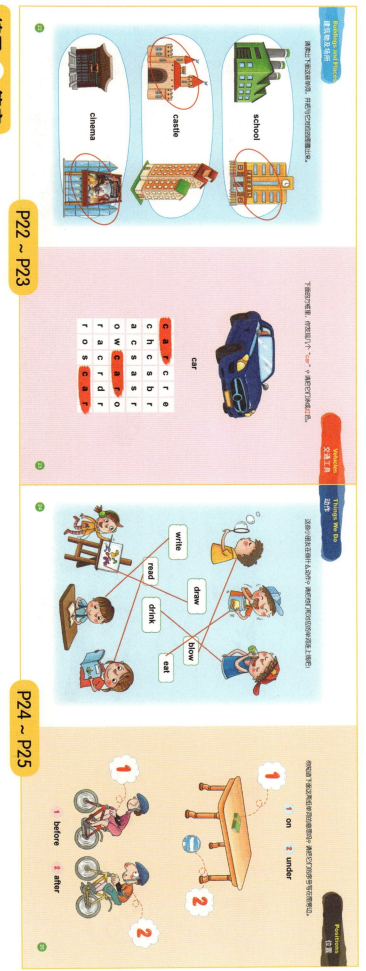

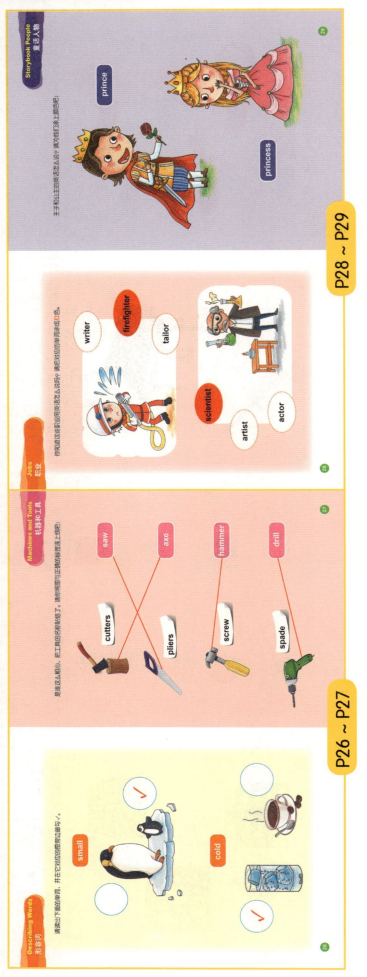
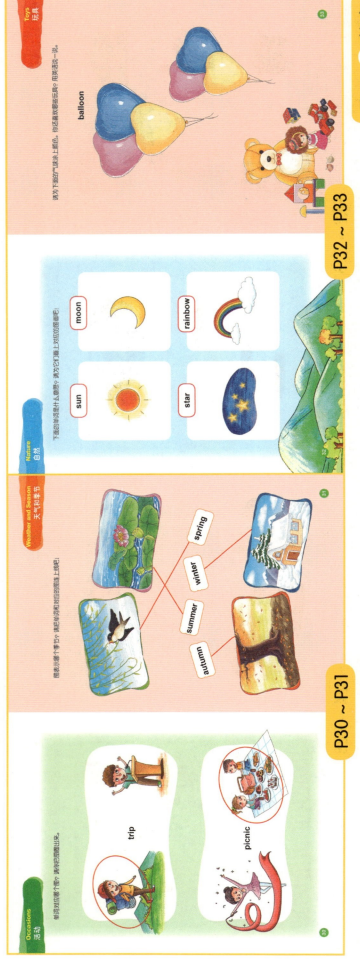

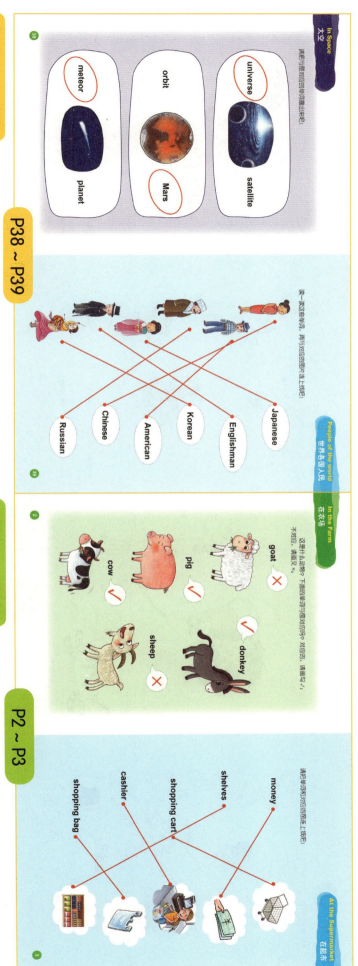

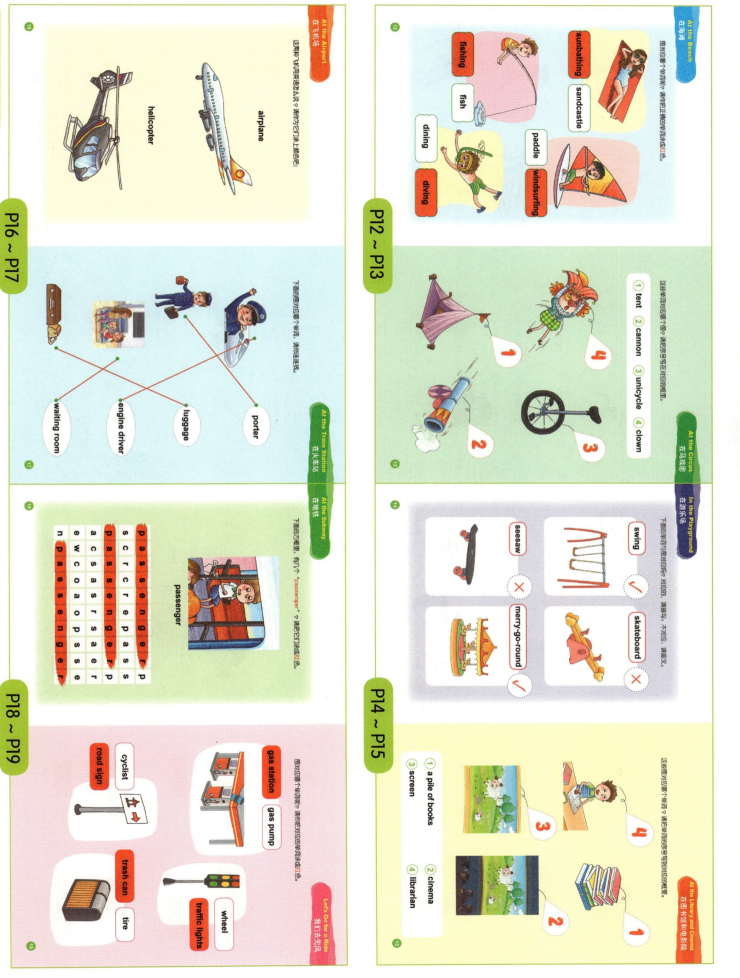

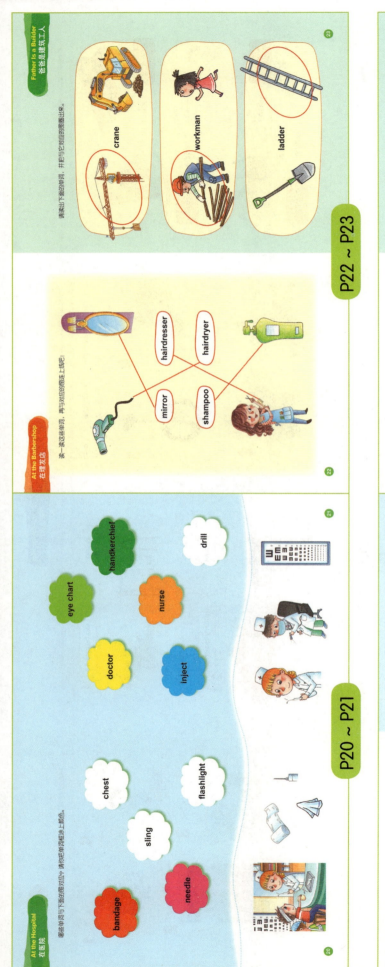

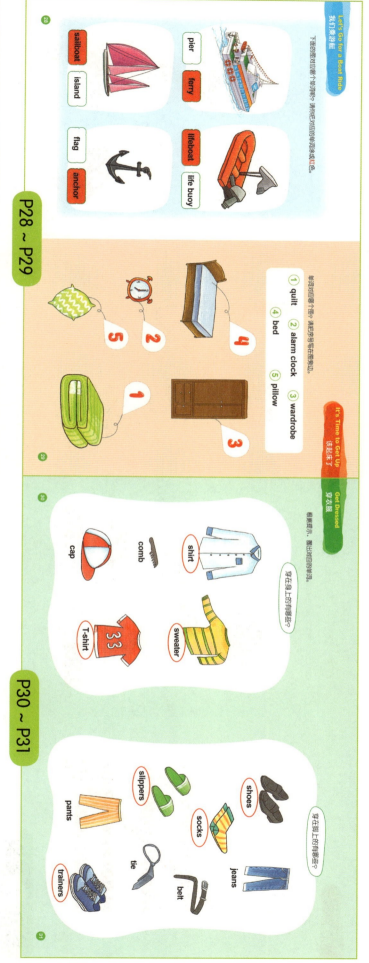
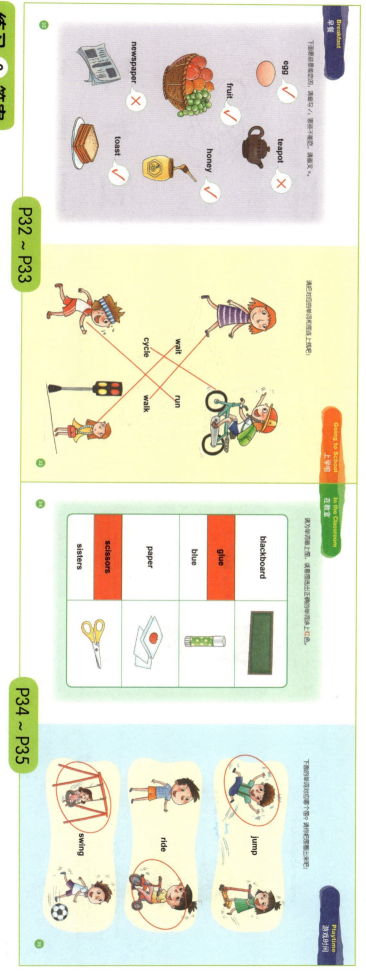

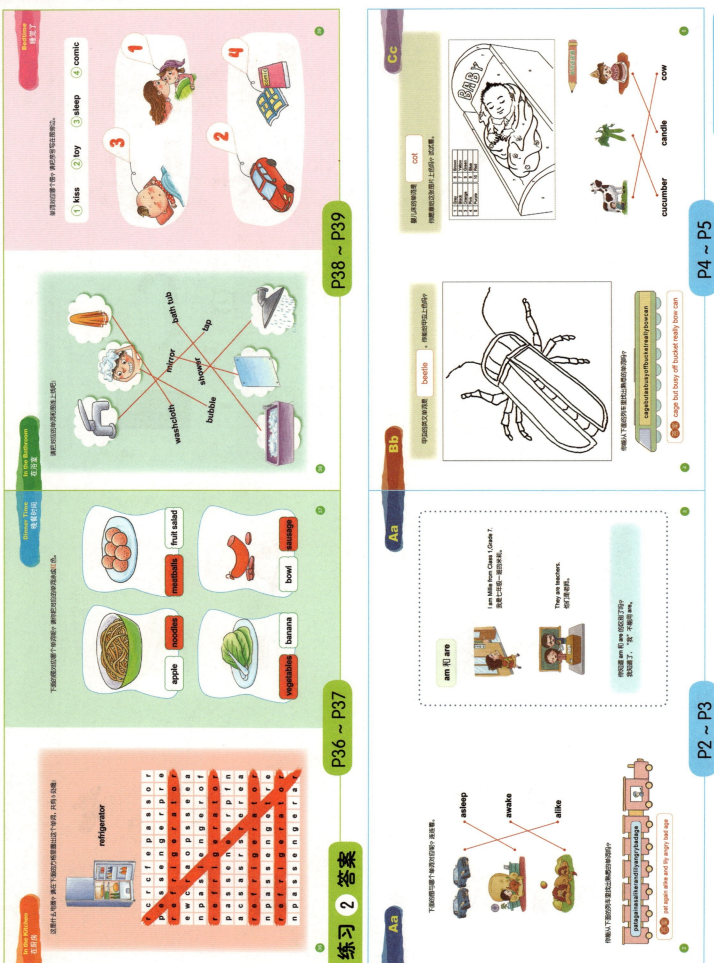

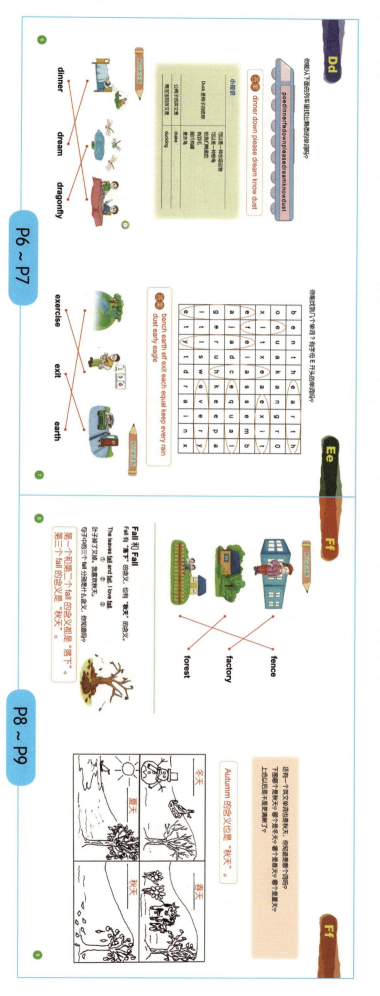

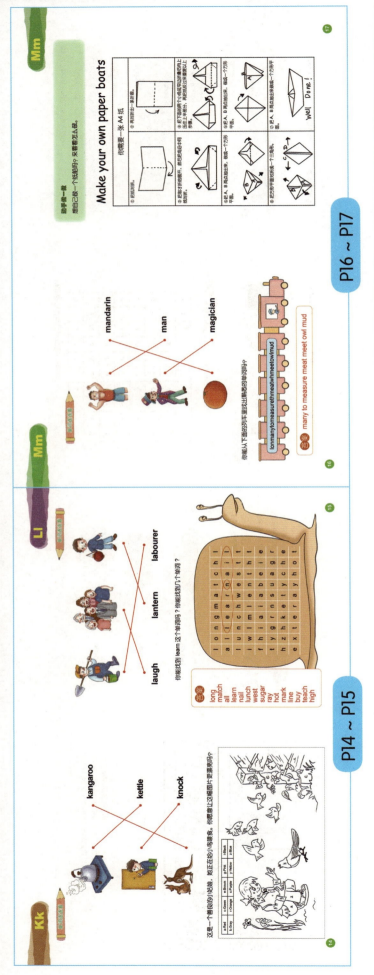
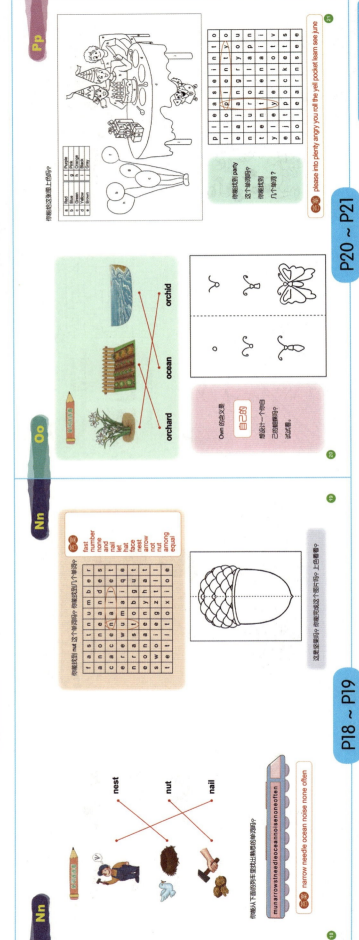

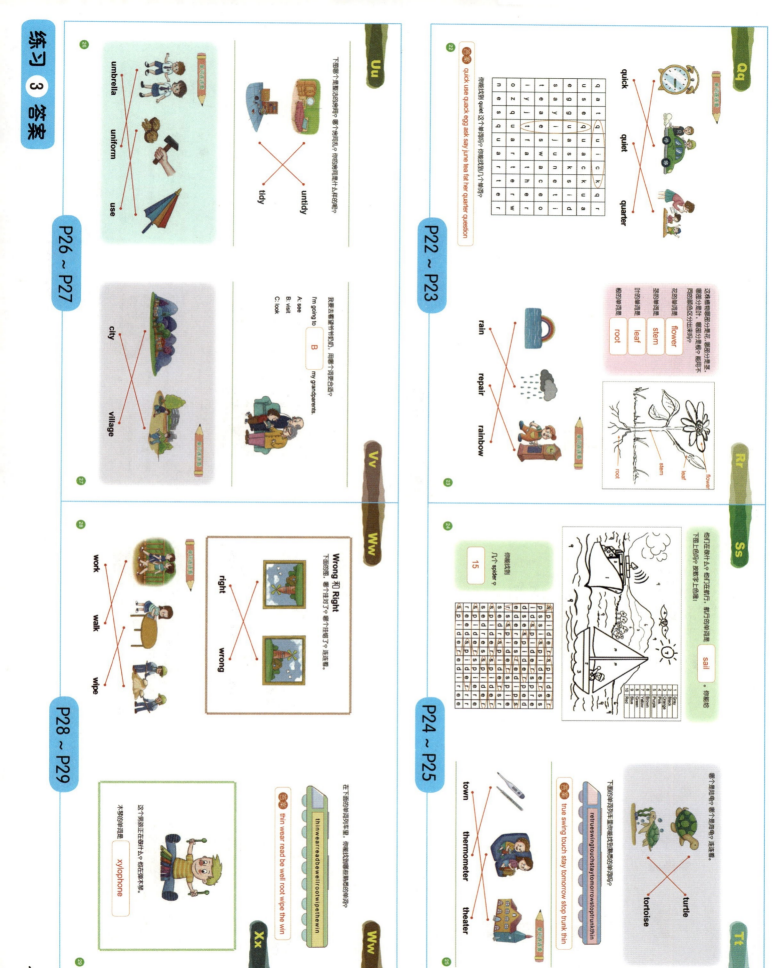

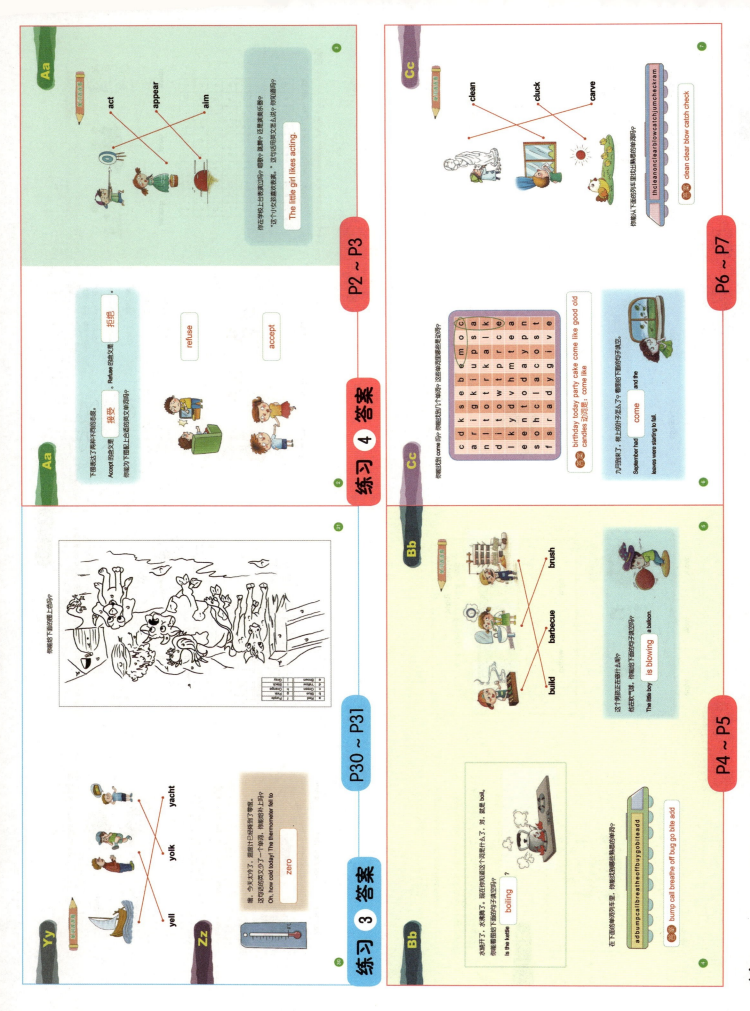

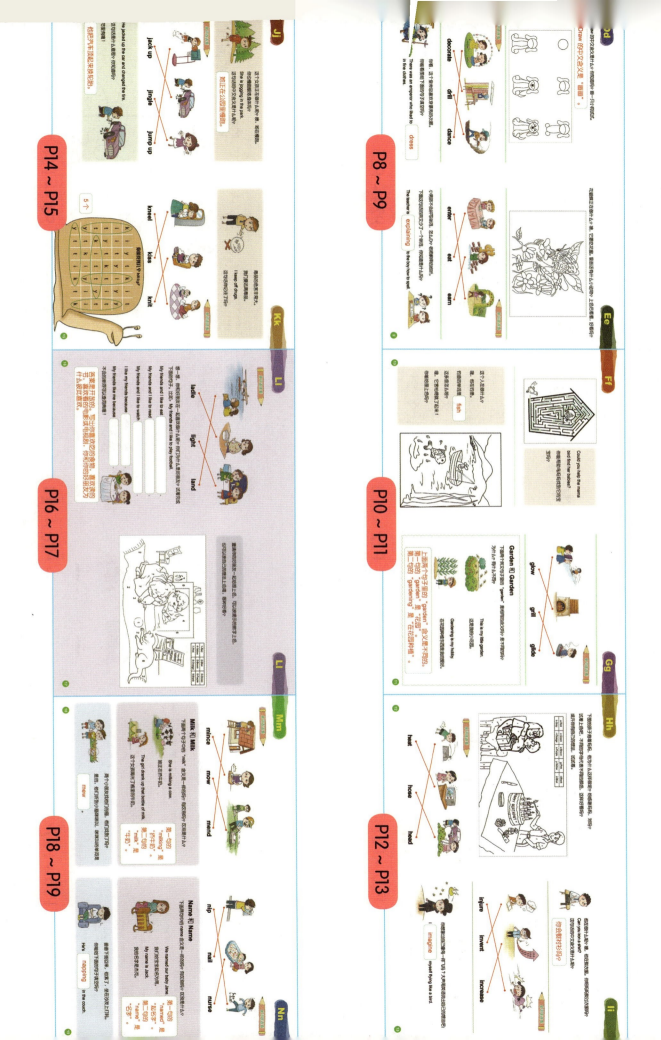

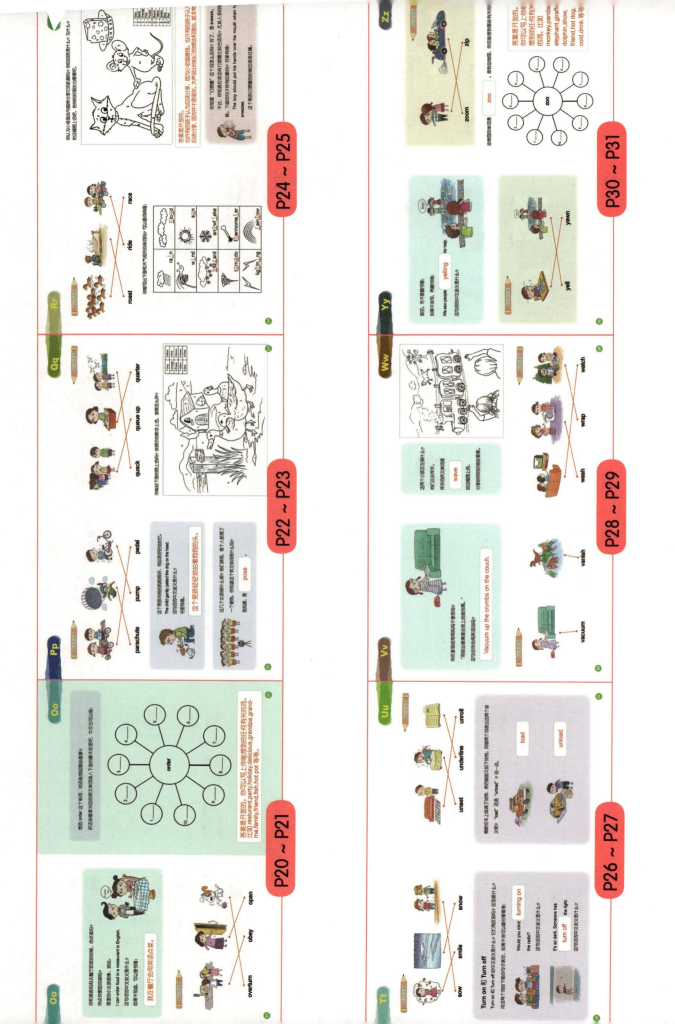

每天5分钟，单词积累不用愁

双语 点读 测评

3~8岁

WORDS for ESL LEARNERS
情景英语4000词

② 场景会话 1000词

沧浪文化英语创研室 ◎ 编著　　戴维·帕特里克·泰奇　王威 ◎ 审订

北京大学出版社
PEKING UNIVERSITY PRESS

使用说明

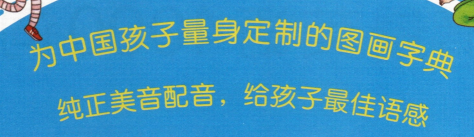

**为中国孩子量身定制的图画字典，
纯正美音配音，给孩子最佳语感**

学 习 单 词　用扫描二维码、下载MP3文件或点读的方式学习单词的正确发音。

图画捉迷藏　孩子观察小图，然后在大图中找到它，并用英语说出来，以此熟悉单词，并提升观察力。

复习场景单词　孩子对单词比较熟悉以后，家长可以和孩子玩"请你说一说"的游戏，如：厨房里面有什么？孩子可以先用中文回答，再用英语复述（家长可适当提醒），最后大家一起玩"图画捉迷藏"游戏，把刚才说的单词在大图中找出来。

内容介绍

场景生动又有趣，积累词汇量，效果 100 分！

Topic 主题
本书共有 34 个主题：在教室、在超市、在动物园、在农场……孩子生活中看到的、应该了解的全都在这里！

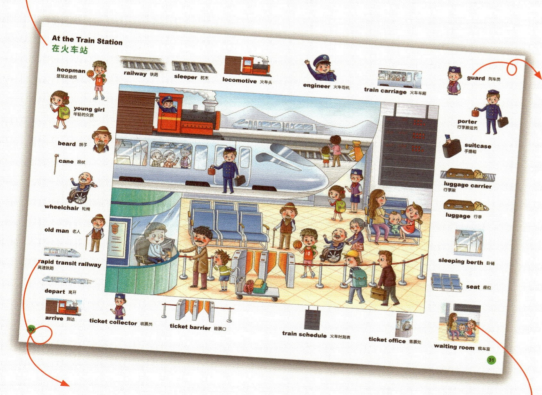

Word 单词
字大突出，一目了然。

Translation 翻译
准确的中文翻译，帮助孩子理解词义。

Illustration 插图
生动的插图，吸引孩子注意力并帮助理解、加深记忆。

音频收听说明

朗读 贝蒂娜·朱莉

美国哥伦比亚大学表演系研究生,为"美语之路"系列图书配音,语音纯正,音质清晰。

语音评测

❶ 扫码 扫描封底的二维码,关注微信公众号。

❷ 语音测评 选择测评内容,开始录音,会有测评分数打出。

扫描二维码

❶ 扫码 扫描封底的二维码,关注"沧浪文化"公众号。

❷ 听音频 点击公众号右下角的"微课和音频",选择收听本书音频。

下载 MP3 文件

❶ 进入官网 百度搜索"沧浪文化书馨网"。

❷ 下载 点击首页右上角的"下载专区",下载本书 MP3 文件。

点读

- 本书支持:"小达人"和"美语之路"点读笔(需另购)。
- 正文四周的文、图,及大图中与小图对应处都可以点读。

❶ 打开电源开关　　❷ 点击封面　　❸ 点读正文中的学习内容

目录 Contents

- 2 在农场
- 4 在超市
- 6 在购物中心
- 8 生日快乐

- 10 今天阳光灿烂
- 12 宠物展览会
- 14 新年和学校音乐会
- 16 在动物园
- 20 在海滩
- 22 在马戏团

- 24 在游乐场
- 26 在图书馆和电影院

- 28 在飞机场
- 30 在火车站
- 32 在地铁
- 34 我们去兜风
- 36 在医院
- 38 在理发店
- 40 爸爸是建筑工人
- 42 叔叔是消防队员
- 44 警察帮助大卫

- 46 清扫院子
- 48 去邮局
- 50 我们乘游艇

- 52 该起床了
- 54 穿衣服

- 56 早餐
- 58 上学啦
- 60 在教室
- 62 游戏时间
- 64 在厨房
- 66 晚餐时间
- 68 在浴室
- 70 睡觉了

In the Farm
在农场

 **fruit tree** 果树  **duckling** 小鸭子  **duck** 鸭子

 **field** 田地

 **hill** 小山

 **farmer** 农夫

 **pigsty** 猪圈

 **hay** 干草

 beehive 蜂箱

 **hen house** 鸡舍

 **pond** 池塘   **turkey** 火鸡  **pig** 猪  **sheep** 绵羊

 bull 公牛
 calf 牛犊
 cow 母牛
 goat 山羊

 rooster 公鸡

 donkey 驴子

 tractor 拖拉机

 barn 谷仓

 farmhouse 农舍

 lamb 小羊羔

 well 井 　　trailer 拖车

At the Supermarket
在超市

shelves 货架

turnstile 十字转门

shopping cart 购物车

beggar 流浪者

pull 拉

lollipop 棒棒糖

doughnut 甜甜圈

customer 顾客

cash register 收款机

give 给

shopping bag 购物袋

olive oil 橄榄油

money 钱币

 a package of cookies 一包饼干

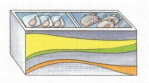 **freezer** 冰柜

 **assistant** 店员

 **checkout counter** 收银台

 cashier 收银员

  bottles of juice 几瓶果汁

 washing powder 洗衣粉

 sack 装进

 pie 派

 **dog food** 狗粮

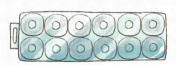 **toilet paper** 卫生用纸

 a bag of rice 一袋米

chicken 鸡肉

5

At the Shopping Centre
在购物中心

 watch 表  **discount** 折扣  **cloth** 布料   **ring** 戒指

shop 商店

elevator 电梯

up 上升

 down 下降

saleswoman 女店员

salesman 男店员

 hamburger 汉堡   **wallet** 钱包   **milkshake** 奶昔

look at 注视　 **mobile phone** 手机　**pen** 笔

 racket 球拍

necklace 项链

 earrings 耳环

tailor 裁缝

 ketchup 番茄酱

fast-food restaurant
快餐店

 **try on** 试穿

staircase
楼梯

 **hot dog** 热狗　 **apple pie** 苹果派　 **French fries** 炸薯条　 **menu** 菜单

7

Happy Birthday
生日快乐

 camera 照相机
 biscuit 饼干
 a box of matches 一盒火柴

 light 点燃

 candle 蜡烛

 birthday cake 生日蛋糕

 scarf 围巾

 present 礼物

 streamers 彩带

 balloon 气球

 jelly 果冻

 hold 抱着

 party game 派对游戏

 **card** 贺卡

 smile 微笑

 party hat 派对帽子

 **kneel** 跪着

 **dance** 跳舞

 **sing** 唱歌

 nuts 果仁

 chocolate 巧克力

 **take a photo** 拍照

 pudding 布丁

 **fruit pie** 水果派

 **blow bubbles** 吹泡泡

 juice 果汁

 candies 糖果

It's Sunny Today
今天阳光灿烂

 pot 花盆    **soil** 泥土   **seeds** 种子

 **washing** 洗好的衣服

 clothes pin 衣夹

 **branch** 树枝

 **trunk** 树干

 **drip** 水滴

 **hanger** 衣架

mower 割草机   **smoke** 烟   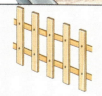 **fence** 篱笆   **paint** 油漆

fertilizer 肥料　 **sun hat** 太阳帽　 **hose** 软管

 **water** 浇水

 **pool** 儿童玩水池

 **rake** 耙子

 **leaves** 树叶

 **grass** 草

 **barbecue grill** 烧烤架

 **tent** 帐篷　 **meat** 肉　 **barbecue** 烧烤　 **fire** 火　**mow** 割草

Pet Show
宠物展览会

pet 宠物

perch 栖木　**chirp** 啾啾叫　**whistle** 吹口哨　**peck** 啄

leash 牵引带

brush 刷

collar 项圈

bone 骨头

nibble 一点点地咬

rabbit 兔子

carrot 胡萝卜

cage 鸟笼

bird 鸟

cricket 蟋蟀

12

basket 篮子

prize 奖品

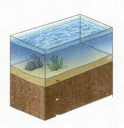
fishbowl 鱼缸

goldfish 金鱼

tortoise 乌龟

bite 咬

white mouse 白鼠

run 跑

jump 跳

butterfly 蝴蝶

parrot 鹦鹉

snail 蜗牛

white mice 多只白鼠

New Year and School Concert
新年和学校音乐会

New Year 新年　　**drum** 鼓　　**drumsticks** 鼓槌

stage 舞台

bow 鞠躬

curtsy 屈膝礼

princess 公主

prince 王子

fairy 仙女

Santa Claus 圣诞老人

dance 跳舞　　**superman** 超人　　**Kung Fu panda** 功夫熊猫　　**clap** 鼓掌

tambourine 铃鼓

 triangle 三角铁

 **music score** 乐谱

 **piano** 钢琴

 **keys** 琴键

 **xylophone** 木琴

 **audience** 观众

soldier 士兵

humpty dumpty 蛋形矮胖子

 wave 挥手

 ninja 忍者

 peep 偷看

wand 魔杖

 cry 哭

At the Zoo
在动物园

giraffe 长颈鹿

horns 角

camel 骆驼

ride 骑

orang-utan 红毛猩猩

zookeeper 动物园管理员

peahen 雌孔雀

flap 拍打

howl 嗥叫

leopard 豹子

chest 胸

peacock 雄孔雀

waterfall 瀑布

16

 **spots** 斑点
 **wolf** 狼
 bars 栏杆
 **zebra** 斑马

 **hippopotamus** 河马

 **crocodile** 鳄鱼

 **lion** 狮子

 cub 幼兽

 ← **mane** 鬃毛

 **sleep** 睡觉

 **beak** 鸟嘴
 kingfisher 翠鸟
 tail 尾巴
tiger 老虎

17

At the Zoo
在动物园

snake 蛇

tongue 舌头

monkey 猴子

panda 熊猫

elephant 大象

headstand 倒立

pigeon 鸽子

chick 小鸡

hen 母鸡

suck 吮吸

parrot 鹦鹉

black 黑色

entrance 入口

 **bridge** 桥
 **pool** 水塘
 wing 翅膀
 feather 羽毛
 **hedgehog** 刺猬

 **goose** 鹅

 **geese** 鹅（复数）

 **flamingo** 火烈鸟

 **rock** 岩石

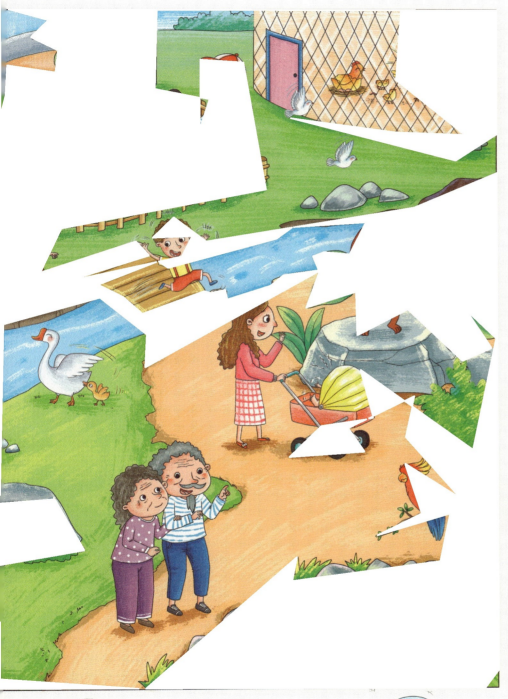

red-crowned crane 丹顶鹤

 **exit** 出口
aviary 鸟舍
 **swan** 天鹅

At the Beach
在海滩

 Frisbee 飞盘   **hermit crab** 寄居蟹   **shell** 贝壳

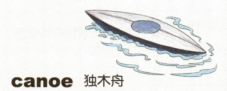
canoe 独木舟

paddle 划桨

snorkel 通气管

flippers 脚蹼

diving 潜水

sandcastle 沙堡

fishing 钓鱼

 **fishing rod** 钓鱼竿    **fish** 鱼   **crab** 螃蟹

stick 树枝
 starfish 海星
 **pebbles** 鹅卵石

beach umbrella 太阳伞

suntan lotion 防晒露

sunglasses 太阳镜

lifesaver 救生员

sunbathing 日光浴

windsurfing 帆板运动

 **fishing net** 渔网

waves 浪

sea 海

At the Circus
在马戏团

 **happy** 快乐的

 sad 悲伤的

 **horse** 马

 **roller coaster** 过山车

 **rock climbing** 攀岩

 rock-climber 攀岩者

 sky wheel 摩天轮

 cotton candy 棉花糖

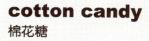 **popcorn** 爆米花

 **high** 高的

 low 低的

trapeze 吊架

 **tent pole** 帐篷杆

 **tent** 帐篷

 **ringmaster** 马戏团领班

 **unicycle** 单轮自行车

 **spectator** 观众

 top hat 大礼帽

 **trapeze artist** 空中飞人

 **rope** 绳梯

 **cannon** 大炮

 whip 鞭子

 clown 小丑

circus ring 马戏场

In the Playground
在游乐场

 grasshopper 蚱蜢　 caterpillar 毛虫　 bee 蜜蜂

 climbing frame 攀登架

 skateboard 滑板

 skipping rope 跳绳

 roller skates 滚轴溜冰鞋

 skip 跳绳

bench 长椅

marbles 弹珠

 hopscotch 跳房子游戏

 bat 球棒　 push 推　pull 拉　 through 通过

 **web** 蜘蛛网　　**swing** 秋千　　**kite** 风筝　　**ball** 球

 **fountain** 喷水池

 **flowerbed** 花坛

 **climb** 攀爬

 **hop** 单脚跳

 **talk** 说话

 **merry-go-round** 旋转木马

slide 滑梯

 chase 追　　 **down** 下　　**up** 上　　 **seesaw** 跷跷板

25

At the Library and Cinema
在图书馆和电影院

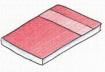 **cover** 封面

 **page** 页

earphone 耳机

 **line** 排队

 **stamp** 盖章

 **librarian** 图书管理员

 **a pile of books** 一堆书籍

 **copy** 抄写

 upside down 颠倒

 **rocket** 火箭

 **desk** 书桌

screen 屏幕

poster 海报

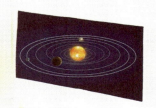
solar system 太阳系

computer 电脑

step stool 梯凳

pop-up book 立体书

big book 大书

cinema 电影院

speaker 音箱

chips 薯条

animated cartoon 动画片

At the Airport
在飞机场

control tower 机场指挥塔

tail 机尾

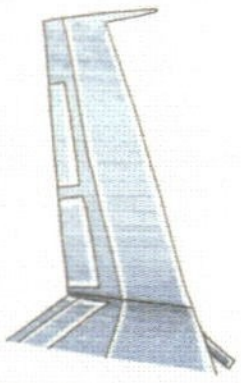

wing 机翼

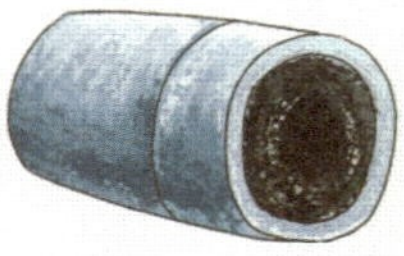

jet engine 喷气式发动机

airplane 飞机

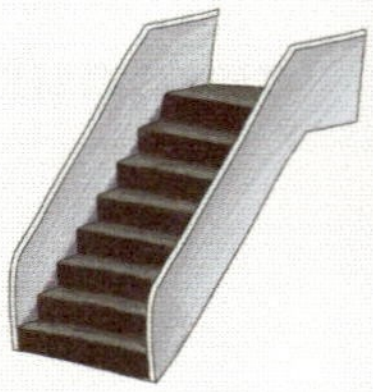

stairs 阶梯

stewardess 空姐

fuel hose 输油管

food truck 食品车

baggage cart 行李运输车

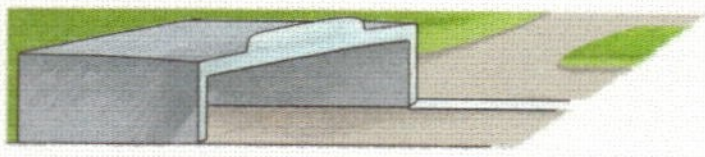

hangar 飞机库

traveller 旅客

Arab 阿拉伯人

Inuit 因纽特人

 **pilot** 飞机驾驶员
 **helicopter** 直升机
 **propeller** 螺旋桨
 **security staff** 安检人员
 **airport bus** 机场巴士
 **take off** 起飞
 **land** 降落
 **security check** 安全检查
 check-in counter 登机柜台
 **automatic ticket barrier** 自动验票处
 **waiting hall** 候机厅

 Mongolian 蒙古人
 runway 跑道
 African 非洲人
 **earmuffs** 耳罩
controller 信号员

At the Train Station
在火车站

hoopman 篮球运动员

young girl 年轻的女孩

beard 胡子

cane 拐杖

wheelchair 轮椅

old man 老人

rapid transit railway 高速铁路

depart 离开

arrive 到达

 **railway** 铁路　**sleeper** 枕木

 **locomotive** 火车头

ticket collector 收票员

ticket barrier 验票口

30

 **engine driver** 火车司机
 **train carriage** 火车车厢
 guard 列车员
 **porter** 行李搬运员
 suitcase 手提箱
 **luggage carrier** 行李架
 **luggage** 行李
 **sleeping berth** 卧铺
 **seat** 座位
 **waiting room** 候车室

 train schedule 火车时刻表   **ticket office** 售票处

At the Subway
在地铁

sliding door 滑门

carriage 车厢

tunnel 隧道

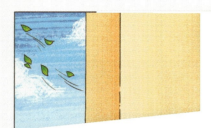

open 开的

close 关的

tourist 游客

map 地图

escalator 电动扶梯

sign 指示牌

backpack 双肩包

 train 列车

 headlight 车头灯

 platform 月台

 passenger 乘客

 glasses 眼镜

 wear a suit 穿着西服

shopping bag 购物袋

 hold 握住

 vomit 呕吐

 walkman 随身听

 briefcase 公文包

 iPad 苹果平板电脑

Let's Go for a Ride
我们去兜风

 stand up 站立　 **scream** 惊呼　 **trash can** 废物箱　 **drill** 钻孔

 **container truck** 货柜车

 **sports car** 跑车

 **taxi** 出租车

 cyclist 骑自行车的人

 **bus stop** 公共汽车站

 **bus** 公共汽车

 **get on** 上车

 **get off** 下车

sit down 坐下

mechanic 修理工

 wheel 车轮

 steering wheel 方向盘

 **gas station** 加油站

 newsstand 书报摊

card reader 读卡器

tire 轮胎

handle 扶手

 bus driver 公共汽车司机

 double-decker bus 双层巴士

footbridge 人行天桥

road sign 路标

 pedestrian 行人

 worker 工人

 motorcycle 摩托车

 traffic lights 交通灯

 garage 汽车修理厂

 attendant 服务员

gas pump 加油器

 car wash 洗车处

At the Hospital
在医院

handkerchief 手帕

medicine 药

chest 胸部

thermometer 体温计

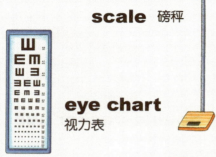
scale 磅秤

eye chart 视力表

sling 吊腕带

bandage 绷带

plaster 创可贴

cotton wool 药棉

flashlight 手电筒

stethoscope 听诊器

nurse 护士

doctor 医生

rubber gloves 橡胶手套

mask 口罩

36

needle 针
 **syringe** 注射器
 inject 打针
 **waiting room** 候诊室

 **patient** 病人

 **bench** 长沙发椅

 **dentist** 牙医

 **dental nurse** 牙科护士

 **dentist chair** 牙科椅

 **dentist light** 牙科无影灯

 **drill** 牙钻

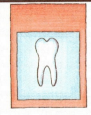 **toothache** 牙痛

 tooth 牙齿

mouth mirror 口镜

At the Barbershop
在理发店

hairdresser 理发师

hood 头罩   **hairdryer** 吹风机

sneeze 打喷嚏

 yellow 黄色

blue 蓝色

 white 白色

 pink 粉色

green 绿色

 **red** 红色

rainy 下雨的

windy 刮风的

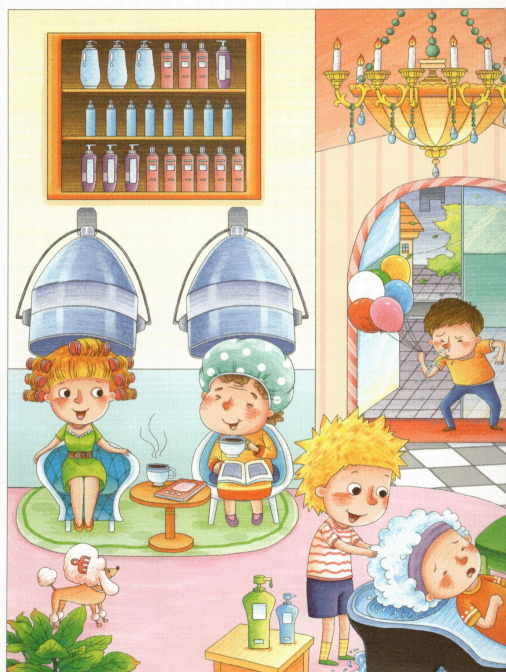

 sink 洗脸盆

 shampoo 洗发露

 **mirror** 镜子
 cape 短披肩
 curler 卷发夹
 **hair** 头发

 **bangs** 刘海

 **dry** 干的

 **wet** 湿的

 **short** 短的

long 长的

 **curly** 卷曲的

 perm 烫发
 **hairdressing** 美发
 **straight** 直的

Father Is a Builder
爸爸是建筑工人

 **crane** 起重机

 hook 吊钩

 **cement mixer** 混凝土车

 **tell** 告诉

 **danger warning sign** 危险警告牌

 **engineer** 工程师

shake hands 握手

plan 设计图

 **metal bar** 钢条

 **drum** 鼓状桶

 **shovel** 铲子

 ladder 梯子

 bricks 砖

 **excavator** 挖土机

 **rubble** 瓦砾

 **dump truck** 自动卸货卡车

 **sand** 沙子

 **workman** 工人

 safety helmet 安全帽

 **scaffolding** 脚手架

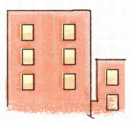 **building** 建筑物

 a plank of wood 一块木板

 **pipe** 管子

 **bags of cement** 多袋水泥

Uncle Is a Fireman
叔叔是消防队员

flames 火焰

tall building 高层建筑

lower one's head 低头

injured person 受伤的人

first-aid kit 急救药箱

stretcher 担架

ambulance 救护车

warning line 警戒线

oxygen tank 氧气筒   axe 斧头   megaphone 扩音器

 **cry for help** 大声呼救
 **smoke** 烟
 **fire engine** 消防车

 spray water 喷水

 **horn** 警报器

 hydrant 消防栓

 nozzle 喷嘴

 **fire extinguisher** 灭火器

 spotlight 聚光灯

 **mask** 防毒面具
 helmet 消防帽
 fireman's outfit 消防衣

 **firemen** 消防队员（复数）

43

Police Officers Help David
警察帮助大卫

police station 警察局　policewoman 女警察

shock 震惊

shop 商店

masked robber 蒙面盗贼

jewelry 珠宝

seat belt 安全带

lamp post 路灯柱

touring car 房车

truck 货车

phone 电话　 lost 丢失　 policeman 男警察　 walkie-talkie 对讲机

  cap 警帽

 handcuffs 手铐

 buttons 纽扣

 police car 警车

 alarm lamp 警灯

 mittens 连指手套

 cross 穿过　 report book 记录本　 traffic police officer 交通警察

Cleaning Courtyard
清扫院子

 **fly** 飞

 broom 扫把

 **pick up** 拾起

a pile of sticks 一堆树枝

 **run away** 逃走

 **stir up a honeycomb** 捅蜂窝

 **line up** 排队

 **corn** 玉米粒

ant 蚂蚁

 **bark** 吠

 **throw** 扔掉

shout 呼喊

 trash can 垃圾桶

lawn 草坪

fallen leaves 落叶　　**courtyard** 院子

garbage truck 垃圾车

sanitation worker 清洁工人

overalls 背带裤

boots 长靴

gloves 手套

heavy 重的

light 轻的

edge 路边　　**litter** 垃圾　　**rubbish** 废弃物　　**overtake** 超车

Going to the Post Office
去邮局

 **post office** 邮局
 mailbox 邮箱
 **mail** 邮寄

 **locate** 定位

 **bicycle** 自行车

 **letterbox** 信箱

 **mailbag** 邮袋

 key 钥匙

 box 箱子

 **scooter** 小型摩托车

 **ship** 船
 **wait** 等待
 **slow** 慢的

envelope 信封 **stamp** 邮票  **letter** 信

 **postal van** 邮车

 **packet** 邮包

 package 包裹

 cardboard 纸箱

 **postman** 邮递员

 **carry** 搬运

 **horse rider** 骑手

 **grassland** 草原

Let's Go for a Boat Ride
我们乘游艇

ferry 渡轮

lifeboat 救生艇

cabin 船舱

sailboat 帆船

row 划船

container ship 货柜船

goggles 护目镜

swimming cap 游泳帽

swimming trunks 游泳裤

swimsuit 游泳衣

swimming race 游泳竞赛

splash 泼水

swimmer 游泳者

stopwatch 秒表

coach 教练

 **deck** 甲板
 rope 绳索
 **flag** 旗帜
 pilot 舵手
 **steering wheel** 舵

 **sailor** 海员

 life buoy 救生圈

 **rail** 围栏

 **anchor** 锚

 **island** 岛屿

 **pier** 码头

 **seagull** 海鸥

dolphin 海豚

 **buoy** 浮标

 **lighthouse** 灯塔

It's Time to Get Up
该起床了

 **baby** 宝宝

 **Susan** 苏珊

 **David** 大卫

 **bedroom** 卧室

 **door** 门

 **bed cover** 床单

 **bed** 床

 **mattress** 床垫

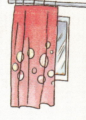 **curtain** 窗帘

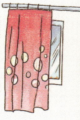 **wardrobe** 衣橱

 pillow 枕头

 quilt 被子

 alarm clock 闹钟

 **drawer** 抽屉

 **mother** 妈妈
 father 爸爸
 **lamp** 灯
 **stretch** 伸懒腰
 nightgown 睡袍
 **pajamas** 睡衣裤
 **cot** 婴儿床
 a vase of flowers 一瓶花
 **picture** 画
 **fan** 风扇

 **sofa** 沙发
 **tea table** 茶几
 **tissues** 纸巾
 **rug** 小地毯

Get Dressed
穿衣服

jacket 外套

tie 领带

tie 领带 diaper 尿布

take off 脱下

pants 裤子

dress 连衣裙

jeans 牛仔裤

T-shirt T恤

put on 穿上

shoes 鞋子

cap 帽子

shorts 短裤

socks 短袜

 **slippers** 拖鞋

 comb 梳子

 **stool** 凳子

dressing table 梳妆台

 **shirt** 男式衬衫

 **blouse** 女式衬衫

 **pantyhose** 裤袜

panties 女式短裤

 **skirt** 裙子

 **trainers** 运动鞋

 **sweater** 毛衣

 belt 腰带

Breakfast
早餐

 vapor 水蒸气

 exhaust hood 抽油烟机 **Thermos** 热水壶

 **stove** 炉灶

 **oven** 烤箱

 **cupboard** 碗柜

 **saucepan** 有柄平底锅

 teapot 茶壶

 kettle 水壶

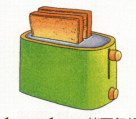 **toaster** 烤面包机

 **toast** 烤面包片

 a pitcher of juice 一壶果汁

56

newspaper 报纸
 **butter** 黄油
 **pour** 倒出
 **honey** 蜂蜜

 **milk** 牛奶

 egg 鸡蛋

 **fruit** 水果

 **cereal** 谷类食物

 **sugar** 糖

 **bread** 面包

 **a mug of coffee** 一杯咖啡
 coffee pot 咖啡壶
a jar of jam 一瓶果酱

57

Going to School
上学啦

 helmet 头盔  school bag 书包   water bottle 水壶

 road 马路

 sidewalk 人行道

 zebra crossing 斑马线

 curb 路边石

 school bus 校车

 gate 大门

car 汽车

broom 扫帚

tree 树

bicycle 自行车

friend 朋友

 **wave** 挥手
 peach 桃子
 basketball 篮球
 **string bag** 网兜

 walk 步行

 **wait** 等候

 **stroller** 婴儿车

 **yawn** 打哈欠

 **street sweeper** 清洁工人

 **sweep** 扫

 **cycle** 骑自行车
 **run** 跑
 **flower** 花
swallow 燕子
speed bump （黄黑条）减速路障

In the Classroom
在教室

 **blackboard** 黑板   **fish tank** 鱼缸    **paper** 纸张

 **chart** 图表

 glue 胶水

 **window** 窗户

 **teacher** 老师

 **color** 填色

 **read** 读

story book 故事书

 painting 绘画    **paints** 颜料   **brush** 画笔   **label** 标签

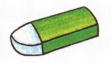 **eraser** 橡皮
 **scissors** 剪刀
 wastepaper basket 废纸篓
 **cut** 剪

 **bookcase** 书架

 crayons 蜡笔

 **easel** 画架

 **shapes** 形状

 paste 粘贴

 **look around** 东张西望

 letters 字母

 pencil 铅笔

 chair 椅子
 listen 听
 write 写
 table 桌子

Playtime
游戏时间

 sand 沙子　 worm 虫子　 dig 挖掘　 boat 小船

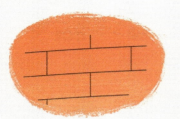 wall 墙

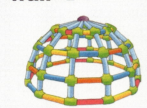 jungle gym 攀登架

 tricycle 三轮车

 cart 手拉车

 scooter 踏板车

 hoop 大圈

 football 足球

 build 建造

 box 盒子

 play dough 橡皮泥　 toy car 玩具车　 spade 铲子

 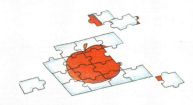

blow 吹　　**funnel** 漏斗　　**swing** 摇荡　　**jigsaw puzzle** 拼图

 **climb** 爬

 **jump** 跳

 **kick** 踢

 **blocks** 积木

 **ride** 骑

 sieve 筛子

 **doll** 洋娃娃

 **puppet** 木偶

shape 模子　　**roll** 擀薄　　**knife** 刀　　**rolling pin** 擀面杖

In the Kitchen
在厨房

 brush 刷子

 apron 围裙

 **dustpan** 簸箕

burner 炉灶

 **knob** 旋钮

 **wok** 锅

dishwashing liquid
洗涤剂

 **sink** 洗涤槽

 **kitchen cloth** 抹布

 **socket** 插座

cherries 樱桃

cupcake tray 杯形蛋糕盘

 **wooden spoon** 木勺

64

 **baking tray** 烘烤盘
 laundry basket 洗衣篮
plug 插头
 **mop** 拖把
 **mixing bowl** 搅拌碗
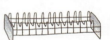 **stack up** 摞起
 **dish rack / drying rack** 碗碟架

 **washing machine** 洗衣机
 tin 罐头
 **flour** 面粉
 watching 观察
refrigerator 冰箱

Dinner Time
晚餐时间

noodles 面条

meatballs 肉丸

fruit salad 水果沙拉

ice cream 冰激凌

apple 苹果

sausage 香肠

carry 端着

tablecloth 桌布

spoon 勺子　　knife 餐刀　　fork 叉子　　bowl 碗

napkin 餐巾　　cat food 猫食　　cat 猫

cup 茶杯
 saucer 茶托
 feed 喂
 set the table 分发餐具

 high chair 婴儿高椅

 chopsticks 筷子

 dish 碟子

 sideboard 餐具柜

 cushion 椅垫

 tray 托盘

 vegetables 蔬菜
 banana 香蕉
 mat 桌垫

In the Bathroom
在浴室

toothbrush 牙刷   **tap** 水龙头   **shower** 淋浴器

bath towel 浴巾

shave 刮胡子

razor 剃刀

basin 洗脸池

mirror 镜子

plug 塞子

washcloth 毛巾

toothpaste 牙膏

shower curtain 浴帘

bubble 泡泡

powder 爽身粉

bath tub 浴缸

toilet 抽水马桶

toilet paper 卫生纸

bathroom scale 浴室体重秤

bathrobe 浴袍

rubber duck 橡皮鸭子

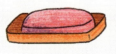
soap 肥皂

sponge 海绵

bath mat 浴室脚垫

potty 儿童便盆

Bedtime
睡觉了

 piggy bank 储蓄罐   **clock** 钟   **photograph** 照片

stars 星星

moon 月亮

 milk bottle 奶瓶

stickers 贴纸

 **bib** 围嘴

mobile 可动挂饰

 **crib** 婴儿床

 **toy** 玩具

 **comic** 漫画书

 switch 开关

 **sleep** 睡觉

70

 **light** 灯光

 hair clip 发卡

 **ribbon** 丝带

 **bookcase** 书柜

 **clothes** 衣服

 **kiss** 吻

 **carpet** 地毯

 board games 棋类游戏

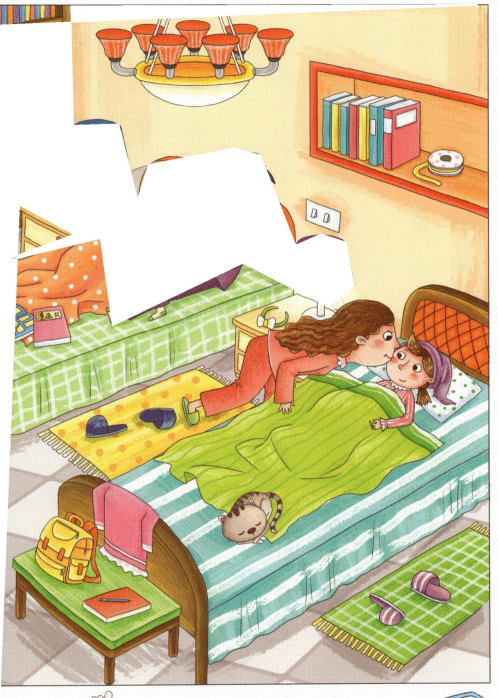

 plant 植物

 **blinds** 百叶窗

 **telephone** 电话

每天5分钟，单词积累不用愁

WORDS for ESL LEARNERS
情景英语4000词

① 基础分类 1000词

沧浪文化英语创研室 ◎ 编著　　戴维·帕特里克·泰奇　王威 ◎ 审订

使 用 说 明

为中国孩子量身定制的图画字典

纯正美音配音,给孩子最佳语感

学 习 单 词 　用扫描二维码、下载MP3文件或点读的方式学习单词的正确发音。

复习单个单词 　用"我说你找"的游戏方式帮助孩子复习所学的单词。如妈妈说中文,孩子说出英语并找出书中对应的图画。以此熟悉单词,并提升观察力。

复习分类单词 　孩子对单词都比较熟悉以后,家长可以和孩子玩"请你说一说"的游戏。如请孩子说一说农场动物有哪些。孩子说,家长对照着书看,对了多少,漏掉的是哪些,这样复习,查漏补缺。

内容介绍

分类明确又全面，积累词汇量，效果100分！

Topic 主题
本书共有 38 个主题：动物、家庭、身体、食物和饮品、玩具……孩子应该了解的全都在这里！

Word 单词
字大突出，一目了然。

Translation 翻译
准确的中文翻译，帮助孩子理解词义。

Illustration 插图
生动的插图，吸引孩子注意力并帮助理解、加深记忆。

音频收听说明

朗读 贝蒂娜·朱莉

美国哥伦比亚大学表演系研究生，为"美语之路"系列图书配音，语音纯正，音质清晰。

语音测评

❶ 扫码 扫描封底的二维码，关注微信公众号。

❷ 语音测评 选择测评内容，开始录音，会有测评分数打出。

扫描二维码

❶ 扫码 扫描封底的二维码，关注"沧浪文化"公众号。

❷ 听音频 点击公众号右下角的"微课和音频"，选择收听本书音频。

下载MP3文件

❶ 进入官网 百度搜索"沧浪文化书馨网"。

❷ 下载 点击首页右上角的"下载专区"，下载本书MP3文件。

点读

- 本书支持："小达人"和"美语之路"点读笔（需另购）。
- 正文中的文字和图片都可以点读。

① 打开电源开关　　② 点击封面　　③ 点读正文中的学习内容

目录 Contents

- 2　家庭
- 3　身体
- 4　穿戴衣物
- 6　在屋子里
- 10　在厨房里
- 12　在教室里

- 13　在游乐场
- 14　在医院里
- 15　在花园里

- 16　农场动物
- 18　野生动物
- 22　水生动物
- 24　鸟类
- 27　昆虫
- 28　花和水果
- 30　蔬菜
- 32　食物和饮品
- 34　乐器
- 36　颜色和形状
- 37　数字
- 38　建筑物及场所

- 42　交通工具
- 45　动作
- 52　位置
- 53　形容词
- 56　机器和工具

- 58　职业
- 62　童话人物
- 63　活动
- 64　天气和季节
- 65　自然
- 66　玩具

- 67　心情和态度
- 68　一日内的时间
- 69　星期
- 70　体育项目及竞赛
- 73　太空
- 74　世界各国人民

Family
家庭

mother 母亲
father 父亲
grandmother 祖母
grandfather 祖父

baby 婴儿
sister 姐妹
brother 兄弟

uncle 伯伯，叔叔，舅舅，姑父，姨父

aunt 伯母，婶母，舅母，姑母，姨母

cousin 堂兄弟，表兄弟，堂姐妹，表姐妹

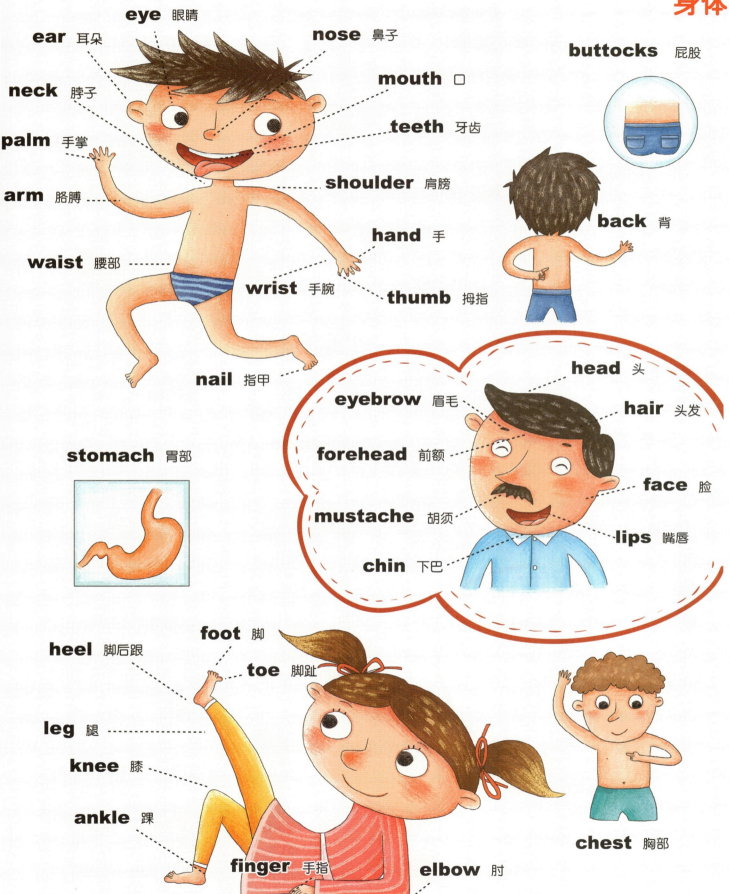

Things We Wear
穿戴衣物

- sweater 毛衣
- ring 戒指，指环
- necklace 项链
- swimsuit 游泳衣
- stockings 长袜
- handkerchief 手帕
- slip 衬裙
- socks 短袜
- blouse 女式衬衫
- nightdress 女式睡衣
- gloves 手套
- shoes 鞋子
- ribbon 丝带
- scarf 围巾
- raincoat 雨衣
- dress 裙子
- T-shirt T恤
- coat 大衣
- slippers 拖鞋
- skirt 短裙
- apron 围裙
- boots 长靴
- pajamas 睡衣裤
- sandals 凉鞋

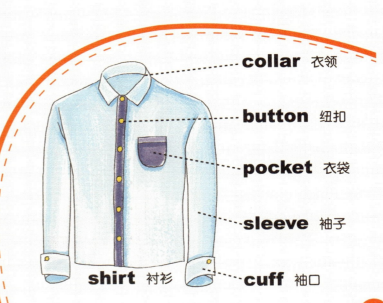

In the House
在屋子里

pillow 枕头

lamp 灯

iron 熨斗

ironing board 熨衣板

bed 床

wardrobe 衣橱

mattress 床垫

bedroom 卧室

photograph 照片

doorbell 门铃

telephone 电话

rug 小地毯

record 唱片

door 门

cot 婴儿床

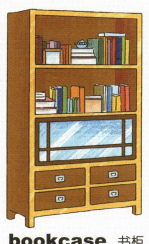

armchair 扶手椅

rattle 拨浪鼓
vase 花瓶

bookcase 书柜

newspaper 报纸

sofa 沙发

carpet 地毯

drawer 抽屉
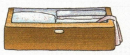

fan 风扇

television 电视

blanket 毛毯

chair 椅子

picture 画

clock 时钟

living room 客厅

umbrella 雨伞

radio 收音机

In the House
在屋子里

tap 水龙头

shower 淋浴器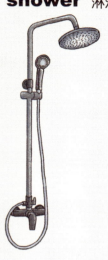

mirror 镜子

heater 热水器

soap 肥皂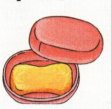

bath tub 浴缸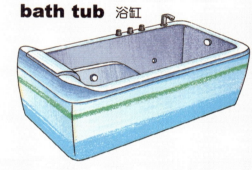

brush 刷子

towel 毛巾

bathroom 浴室

basin 洗脸盆

toilet 抽水马桶

toothpaste 牙膏

toothbrush 牙刷

switch 开关

dining room 餐厅

calendar 日历

ladder 梯子

broom 扫帚

dustbin 垃圾桶

table 桌子

comb 梳子

curtain 窗帘

hairbrush 发梳

tablecloth 餐布

mat 地巾

window 窗户

In the Kitchen
在厨房里

 **saucepan** 有柄平底锅

 glass 玻璃杯

 **bowl** 碗

 **pot** 锅

 **fork** 叉子

kitchen 厨房

 **plate** 盘子

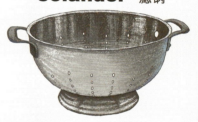 **colander** 滤锅

 **spoon** 勺子

ladle 长柄勺子

 **pan** 煎锅

 **cup** 有柄茶杯

salt 盐

knife 刀子

mug 大杯,马克杯

 **sugar** 糖 **candy** 糖果

 **basket** 篮子

 **bucket** 水桶

- **kettle** 水壶
- **shelf** 架子
- **oven** 烤箱
- **strainer** 筛网
- **can opener** 罐头刀
- **tray** 托盘
- **funnel** 漏斗
- **jar** 大口瓶
- **matches** 火柴
- **mop** 拖把
- **teapot** 茶壶
- **refrigerator** 冰箱
- **jug** 带柄水壶
- **straw** 吸管
- **bottle** 瓶子
- **Thermos** 暖壶
- **sink** 水槽
- **stove** 炉灶
- **rolling pin** 擀面杖

In the Classroom
在教室里

board eraser 板擦

chalk 粉笔

dictionary 字典

pupils 学生

pencil 铅笔

eraser 橡皮

book 书

desk 书桌

glue 胶水

blackboard 黑板

sharpener 铅笔刀

crayon 彩笔, 蜡笔

scissors 剪刀

fountain pen 水笔

pen 笔

ruler 尺子

wastepaper basket 废纸篓

12

In the Playground
在游乐场

seesaw 跷跷板

Ferris wheel 摩天轮

climbing frame 攀登架

swinging ship 海盗船

jump rope 跳绳

merry-go-round 旋转木马

roller coaster 过山车

kite 风筝

skateboard 滑板

swing 秋千

slide 滑梯

bat 球棒

In the Hospital
在医院里

 **plaster cast** 石膏绷带

 **thermometer** 体温计

wheelchair 轮椅

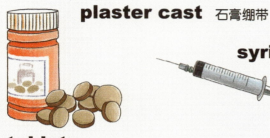 **tablets** 药片

syringe 注射器

 **stethoscope** 听诊器

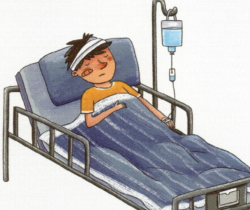 **patient** 病人

 **first-aid kit** 急救药箱

plaster 膏药

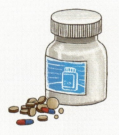 **medicine** 药

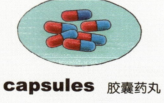 **capsules** 胶囊药丸

 **cotton balls** 药棉

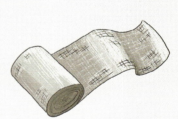 **bandage** 绷带

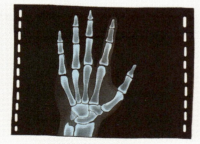 **X-ray** 射线照片

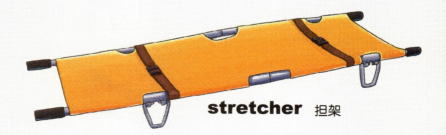 **stretcher** 担架

Farm Animals
农场动物

dog 狗
cat 猫
kitten 小猫
mouse 老鼠

rabbit 兔子

pig 猪

sheep 绵羊
lamb 小绵羊
goat 山羊
kid 小山羊

horse 马

donkey 驴

ox 公牛
cow 母牛
calf 小牛

hen 母鸡
cock 公鸡
chick 小鸡

earthworm 蚯蚓

duckling 小鸭
duck 鸭子
goose 鹅
gosling 小鹅

deer 鹿

monkey 猴子

leopard 豹

snake 蛇

koala 考拉

squirrel 松鼠

lion 狮子

zebra 斑马

horn 角

paw 爪

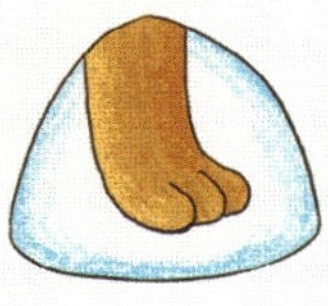

hoof 蹄

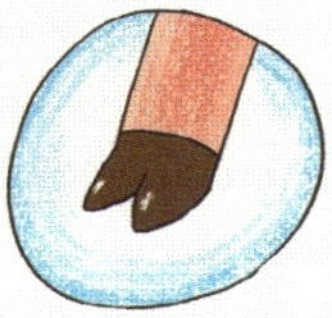

whisker 胡须

Wild Animals
野生动物

gorilla 大猩猩

kangaroo 袋鼠

crocodile 鳄鱼

rhinoceros 犀牛

hamster 仓鼠

bison 野牛

moose 麋鹿

buffalo 水牛

reindeer 驯鹿

porcupine 箭猪

tortoise 乌龟

rat 老鼠

frog 青蛙

lizard 蜥蜴

bat 蝙蝠

chipmunk 金花鼠

snail 蜗牛

hippopotamus 河马

Aquatic Animals
水生动物

sea horse 海马

octopus 章鱼

crab 螃蟹

squid 鱿鱼

walrus 海象

prawn 虾

starfish 海星

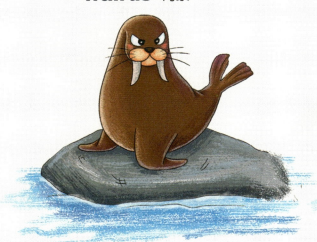

lobster 龙虾

fin 鳍

scales 鱼鳞

Birds
鸟类

bird 鸟

crow 乌鸦

pigeon 鸽子

sparrow 麻雀

penguin 企鹅

swan 天鹅

owl 猫头鹰

magpie 喜鹊

swallow 燕子

peacock 孔雀

Birds
鸟类

cuckoo 布谷鸟

red-crowned crane 丹顶鹤

pelican 鹈鹕，塘鹅

toucan 巨嘴鸟

albatross 信天翁

robin 知更鸟

hummingbird 蜂鸟

kingfisher 翠鸟

flamingo 红鹳

nightingale 夜莺

stork 鹳

Insects 昆虫

butterfly 蝴蝶

beetle 甲虫

bee 蜜蜂

ladybug 瓢虫

cockroach 蟑螂

spider 蜘蛛

flea 跳蚤

cricket 蟋蟀

caterpillar 毛虫

mosquito 蚊子

dragonfly 蜻蜓

ant 蚂蚁

fly 苍蝇

Flowers and Fruits
花和水果

honeydew melon 蜜瓜

watermelon 西瓜

grape 葡萄

cherry 樱桃

mango 芒果

apple 苹果

peach 桃

blackberry 黑莓

grapefruit 葡萄柚

papaya 木瓜

banana 香蕉

plum 李子

coconut 椰子

tomato 番茄

pear 梨

pineapple 菠萝

orange 橙

kiwi fruit 猕猴桃

Vegetables
蔬菜

onion 洋葱

potato 马铃薯

radish 小萝卜

carrot 胡萝卜

bean 豆角

pea 豌豆

pumpkin 南瓜

cabbage 卷心菜

celery 芹菜

cauliflower 菜花

eggplant 茄子

broccoli 西蓝花

leek 大葱

asparagus 芦笋

cucumber 黄瓜

turnip 芜菁

garlic 蒜头

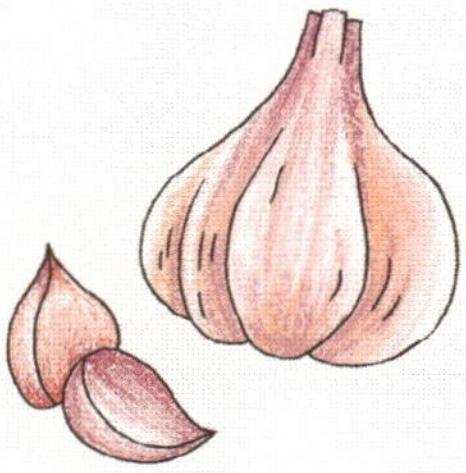

lettuce 生菜

green pepper 青椒

spinach 菠菜

chilli 辣椒

Food and Drinks
食物和饮品

cake 蛋糕

hamburger 汉堡包

sandwich 三明治

doughnut 甜甜圈

pizza 披萨

pie 饼

croissant 牛角面包

bread 面包

toast 吐司，烤面包

cookie 曲奇饼

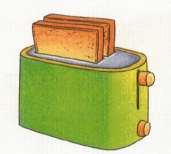

bun 小圆面包

pancake 薄煎饼

salad 沙拉

egg 鸡蛋

spaghetti 意大利面

hot dog 热狗

milk 牛奶

soup 汤

fruit juice 果汁

tea 茶

coffee 咖啡

margarine 人造黄油

jam 果酱

cheese 奶酪

butter 黄油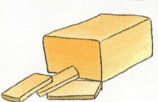

peanut butter 花生酱

meat 肉

chicken 鸡肉

chocolate 巧克力

can 罐头

honey 蜂蜜

sausage 香肠

ice cream 冰激凌

Musical Instruments
乐器

banjo 班卓琴

guitar 吉他

tuba 低音号

triangle 三角铁

cymbal 铙钹

violin 小提琴

piano 钢琴

harmonica 口琴

flute 长笛

Colors and Shapes
颜色和形状

Numbers 数字

 one 一

 two 二

three 三

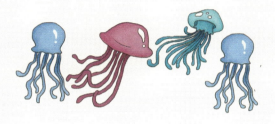 four 四

five 五

 six 六

seven 七

 eight 八

nine 九

 ten 十

eleven 十一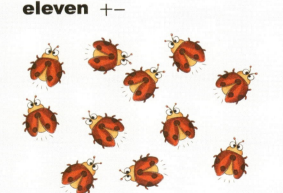

 twelve 十二

Buildings and Places
建筑物及场所

windmill 风车

factory 工厂

church 教堂

airport 飞机场

temple 庙宇

house 房子

library 图书馆

school 学校

fire station 消防局

cinema 电影院

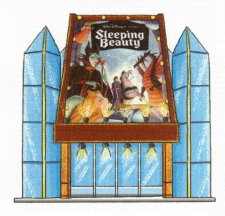

train station 火车站

balcony 阳台

roof 屋顶

apartment 住宅大厦

castle 城堡

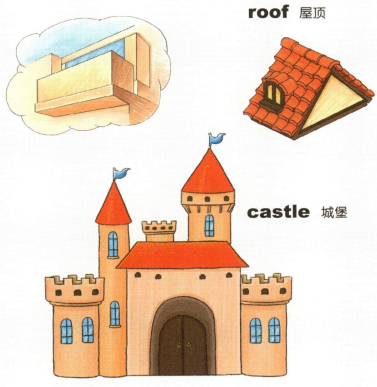

police station 警察局

post office 邮政局

Buildings and Places
建筑物及场所

harbour 海港

zoo 动物园

pier 码头

beach 沙滩

elevator 电梯

swimming pool 游泳池

park 公园

corridor 走廊

office 办公室

department store 百货公司

hotel 酒店

bank 银行

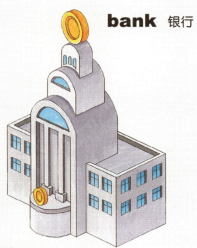

stairs 楼梯

supermarket 超市

cafeteria 自助餐厅

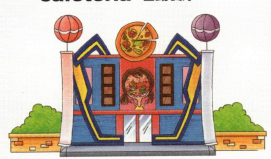

escalator 扶手电梯

museum 博物馆

hospital 医院

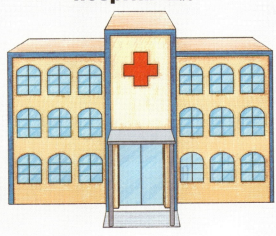

Vehicles
交通工具

car 汽车

motorcycle 摩托车

dump truck 自动卸货卡车

container truck 货柜车

bus 公共汽车

van 厢式货车

jeep 吉普车

fire engine 救火车

tire 轮胎

truck 货车

train 火车

ambulance 救护车

taxi 出租车

railway 铁路

lamp post 路灯柱

helicopter 直升机

traffic lights 交通信号灯

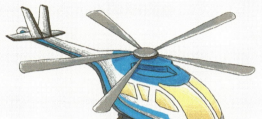

pedestrian crossing 人行横道

zebra crossing 斑马线

jet airplane 飞机

footbridge 人行天桥

underground train 地铁

bicycle 自行车

bridge 桥

Vehicles
交通工具

ship 船

canoe 独木舟

tugboat 拖船

speedboat 快艇

hovercraft 气垫船

gondola 平底船

ferry 渡轮

boat 小船，艇

paddle 桨

lifesaver 救生圈

buoy 浮标

yacht 游艇

submarine 潜水艇

spaceship 太空船

balloon 热气球

parachute 降落伞

rocket 火箭

Things We Do
动作

scrub 擦洗

wash 洗

clap 拍手

kiss 亲吻

pour 倒出

catch 接，抓住

feed 喂

knock 敲

cook 煮

Things We Do
动作

ride 骑

march 前进

point 指向

roll 擀薄

skate 溜冰

sew 缝纫

smell 闻,嗅

slide 滑行

48

shoot 射击

squeeze 挤，压榨

sweep 扫

swim 游泳

swing 荡，摇荡

tear 撕开

throw 抛

wave 挥手

yawn 打哈欠

whistle 吹口哨

Things We Do
动作

hop 单脚跳

fight 打架

dig 挖掘

kick 踢

jog 慢跑

wrap 包起来

run 跑

fall 摔倒

Positions
位置

upside down 倒置

behind 在……后面

in front of 在……前面

between 在……之间

above 在……上面

left 左

right 右

below 在……下面

beside 在……旁边

on 在……之上

out 在……外面

in 在……里面

under 在……之下

before 在……之前

after 在……之后

top 顶

up 向上

down 向下

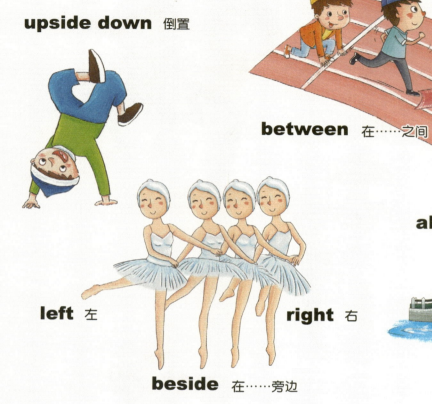
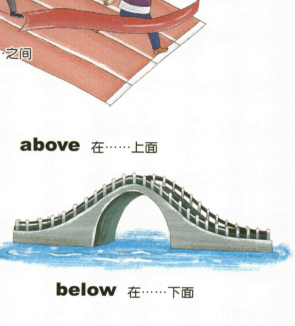
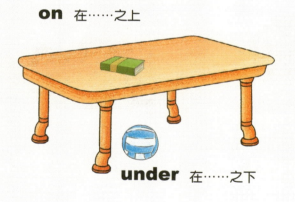

Describing Words
形容词

sick 有病的　　**well** 健康的

light 轻的　　**heavy** 重的

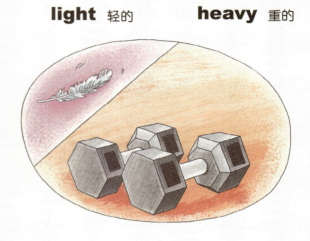

young 年轻的　　**old** 年老的

shallow 浅的　　**deep** 深的

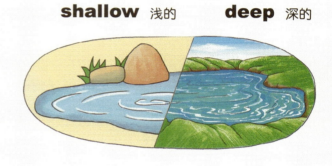

far 远的

near 近的

bright 明亮的

dark 黑暗的

Machines and Tools
机器和工具

bulldozer 推土机

shovel 铁锹

tractor 拖拉机

cement mixer 混凝土车

saw 锯

crane 起重机

axe 斧子

pliers 钳子

drill 钻

wheelbarrow 独轮手推车

56

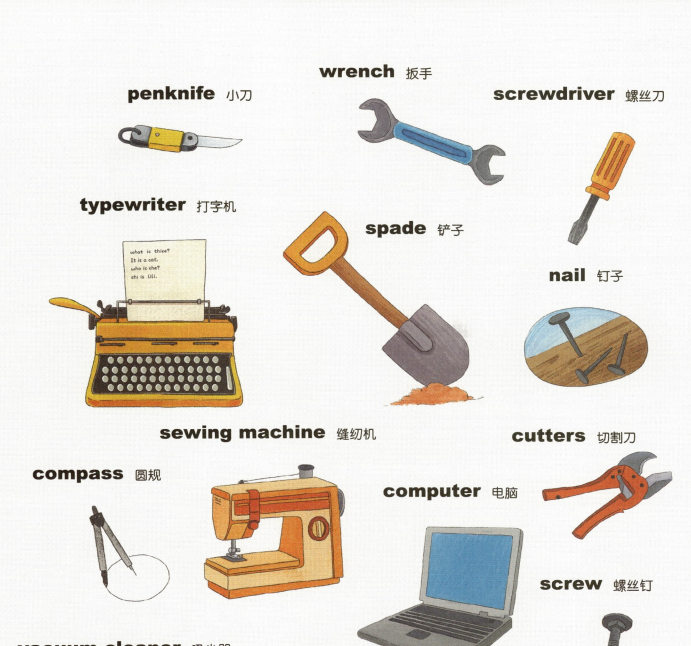

Jobs
职业

baker 面包师傅

actor 男演员

astronaut 宇航员

actress 女演员

bus driver 公共汽车司机

cashier 收银员

carpenter 木匠

butcher 屠夫，肉商

shoemaker 鞋匠

clown 小丑

bus conductor 公共汽车售票员

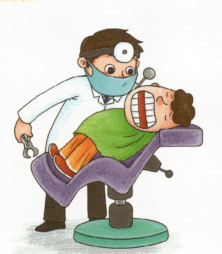
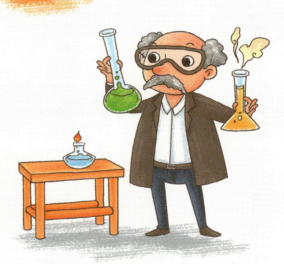

Jobs
职业

gardener 园丁

magician 魔术师

hairdresser 理发师

conductor 指挥

cowboy 牛仔

tailor 裁缝

farmer 农夫

firefighter 消防队员

florist 花店主人

pilot 飞行员

sailor 水手

postman 邮递员

porter 行李搬运员

waitress 女服务员

waiter 男服务员

salesman 男售货员

saleswoman 女售货员

writer 作家

Storybook People
童话人物

Occasions 活动

- trip 旅行
- birthday party 生日会
- barbecue 烧烤
- camping 露营
- wedding 婚礼
- art festival 艺术节
- speech competition 演讲比赛
- sport games 运动会
- picnic 野餐
- summer camp 夏令营

Weather and Season
天气和季节

sunny 天晴的

rainy 下雨的

snowy 下雪的

windy 有风的

cloudy 多云的

lightning 闪电

foggy 有雾的

spring 春

summer 夏

autumn 秋

winter 冬

Nature 自然

Toys 玩具

Rubik's Cube 魔方

blocks 积木

Barbie doll 芭比娃娃

Lego 乐高积木

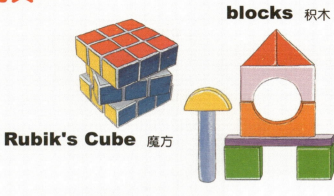

top 陀螺

teddy bear 玩具熊

mask 面具

puppet 木偶

yo-yo 悠悠球

doll 洋娃娃

balloons 气球

marbles 弹珠

jigsaw puzzle 拼图

Feelings and Attitudes
心情和态度

sad 悲伤的

happy 快乐的

glad 高兴的

proud 骄傲的

angry 愤怒的

jealous 妒忌的

frightened 受惊的

selfish 自私的

generous 慷概的

active 活跃的

polite 有礼貌的

helping 爱帮助人的

Times of the Day
一日内的时间

morning 上午

noon 中午

evening 傍晚

night 晚上

---

breakfast 早餐

lunch 午餐

dinner / supper 晚餐

bedtime 就寝时间

Days of the Week
星期

Monday 星期一
Tuesday 星期二
Wednesday 星期三

Thursday 星期四
Friday 星期五
Saturday 星期六
Sunday 星期日

Sports and Games
体育项目及竞赛

Sports and Games
体育项目及竞赛

rowing 划船

surfing 冲浪

heel-and-toe walking race 竞走

swimming 游泳

marathon 马拉松

skiing 滑雪

running 赛跑

table tennis 乒乓球

In Space
太空

satellite 人造卫星

orbit 运行轨道

space station 空间站
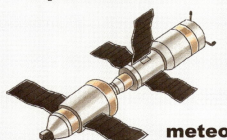

meteor 流星

planet 行星
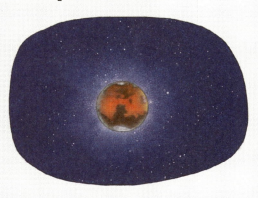

black hole 黑洞

star 恒星
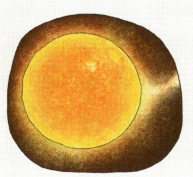

Mars 火星

the Milky Way 银河

universe 宇宙

People of the World
世界各国人民

Chinese 中国人

American 美国人

Russian 俄罗斯人

Englishman 英国人

Japanese 日本人

Italian 意大利人

Egyptian 埃及人

Austrian 奥地利人

Thai 泰国人

Arab 阿拉伯人

Indian 印度人

German 德国人

Singaporean 新加坡人

Canadian 加拿大人

Frenchman 法国人

Korean 朝鲜/韩国人

Mexican 墨西哥人

Greek 希腊人

Spanish 西班牙人

Australian 澳大利亚人

75

WORDS for ESL LEARNERS
情景英语4000词

3~8岁

3 常用字典
1000词

练习册
ACTIVITY BOOK

北京大学出版社
PEKING UNIVERSITY PRESS

下面的图与哪个单词对应呢？连连看。

asleep

awake

alike

你能从下面的列车里找出熟悉的单词吗？

am 和 are

I am Millie from Class 1,Grade 7.
我是七年级一班的米莉。

They are teachers.
他们是老师。

你知道 am 和 are 的区别了吗?
我知道了，"我"不能用 are。

甲虫的英文单词是 _____。你能给甲虫上色吗?

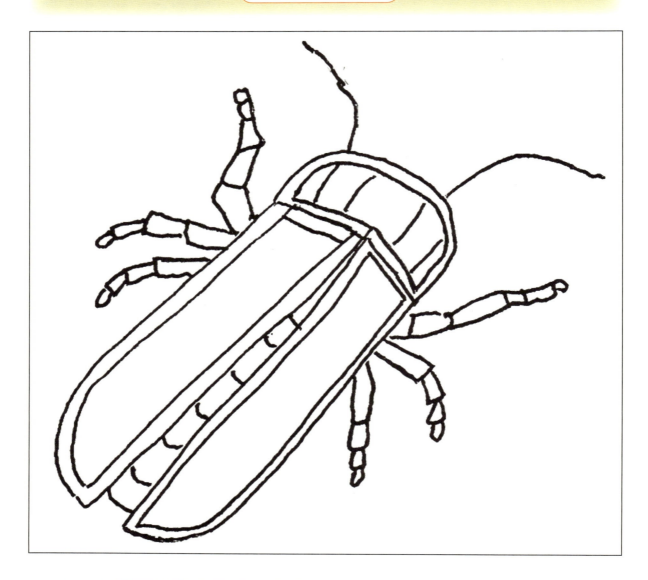

你能从下面的列车里找出熟悉的单词吗?

cagebutasbusyoffbucketreallybowcan

婴儿床的单词是 ▢

你愿意给这张图片上色吗？试试看。

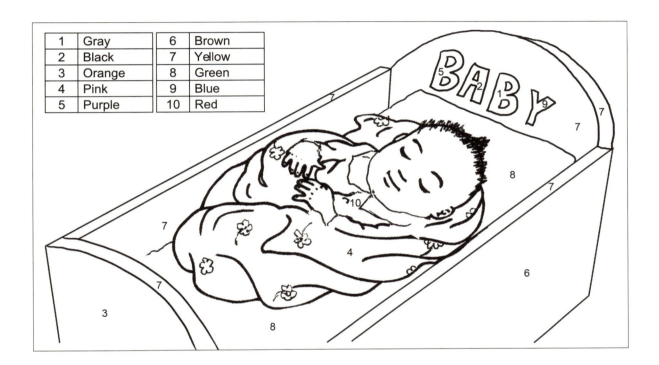

1	Gray	6	Brown
2	Black	7	Yellow
3	Orange	8	Green
4	Pink	9	Blue
5	Purple	10	Red

单词连连看

cucumber   **candle**   **cow**

你能从下面的列车里找出熟悉的单词吗？

poedinnerfedownpleasedreamknowdust

小知识

Duck 是鸭子的统称	可以是一种农场动物 可以是一种野鸟 给我们鸭蛋吃 有羽毛 脚爪有蹼 是水鸟
公鸭子的英文是	drake
鸭宝宝的英文是	duckling

单词连连看

dinner   **dream**   **dragonfly**

你能找到几个单词？有字母 E 开头的单词吗？

b	e	n	t	h	e	a	r	t	h
o	e	u	a	k	a	n	g	r	0
x	l	t	x	e	a	e	x	i	t
e	f	e	i	a	s	s	e	m	b
a	j	a	d	c	e	q	u	a	l
g	e	r	u	h	k	e	e	p	a
l	t	l	s	w	e	v	e	r	y
e	t	y	t	d	r	a	i	n	x

exercise　　　　　**exit**　　　　　**earth**

7

单词连连看

fence

factory

forest

Fall 和 Fall

Fall 有 "**落下**" 的含义，也有 "**秋天**" 的含义。

The leaves fall and fall. I love fall.

叶子掉了又掉。我喜欢秋天。

句子中的三个 fall 分别是什么含义，你知道吗？

还有一个英文单词也是秋天,你知道是哪个词吗?

下图哪个是秋天?哪个是冬天?哪个是春天?哪个是夏天?

上色以后是不是更清晰了?

g	r	o	u	n	d	u	n	n	u	g	o
r	o	u	n	g	r	o	u	n	d	r	u
g	r	o	g	r	o	u	n	d	u	o	n
d	g	g	r	o	u	n	d	g	r	u	o
u	n	d	g	r	o	u	n	d	r	n	u
g	r	o	u	n	d	d	n	u	r	d	o
r	g	r	o	u	n	d	d	u	n	r	d
o	r	u	o	g	r	o	u	n	d	r	u
u	u	r	o	g	r	o	u	n	d	d	r
n	g	r	o	u	n	d	u	n	d	e	r
d	d	d	u	n	o	n	u	g	r	o	n
g	r	o	u	n	d	g	r	o	u	n	d

你能找出几个 ground?

花园的单词是 _____。 上色后再看看吧，是不是很漂亮?

1	Gray
2	Black
3	Orange
4	Pink
5	Purple

6	Brown
7	Yellow
8	Green
9	Blue
10	Red

Help 是什么意思?

你能帮小鸟找到去南方的路吗?

下图的小鸟宝宝是不是饿了?

"饿"的单词是 ▢

想不想给图上色呢?试试看。

a	Red
b	Blue
c	Green
d	Yellow
e	Brown
f	Purple
g	Pink
h	Orange
i	Black
j	Gray

Ii

单词连连看

insect

ill

iron

你能找到几个 insect？

i	n	s	e	c	t	s	e	s	e	s	i
n	i	e	i	n	s	e	c	t	n	s	n
t	i	n	s	e	c	t	e	e	i	e	s
n	i	n	s	e	c	t	s	s	n	i	e
i	n	s	e	c	t	n	e	i	s	n	c
n	s	e	i	n	s	e	c	t	e	i	t
i	n	i	n	s	e	c	t	t	c	t	c
i	n	s	e	c	t	e	e	i	t	i	s
n	i	n	t	e	i	n	s	e	c	t	f
i	n	s	e	c	t	i	n	s	e	c	t
n	s	t	e	c	t	i	n	s	e	c	t
i	n	s	c	e	t	n	n	e	s	t	i

你能完成下面的蜘蛛图吗？

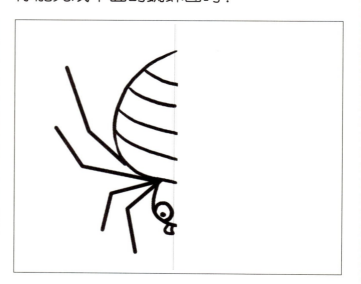

 单词连连看

 jungle

 jeep

 jetty

两个小朋友做什么呢？她们手拉手去上学。你能给这张图上色吗？

Kk

单词连连看

kangaroo

kettle

knock

这是一个善良的小姑娘,她正在给小鸟喂食。你愿意让这幅图片更漂亮吗?

a-Red	c-Green	e-Brown	g-Pink	i-Black
k-Gray	r-Orange	x-Purple	y-Yellow	z-Blue

laugh **lantern** **labourer**

你能找到 learn 这个单词吗？你能找到几个单词？

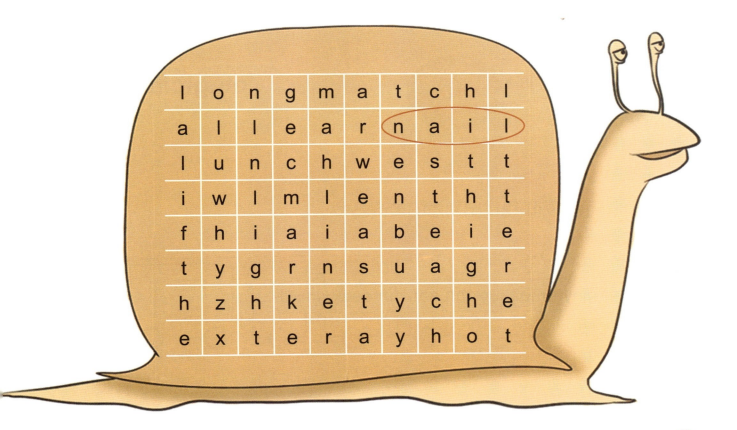

Mm

单词连连看

   mandarin

   man

   magician

你能从下面的列车里找出熟悉的单词吗？

动手做一做

想自己做一个纸船吗?来看看怎么做。

Make your own paper boats

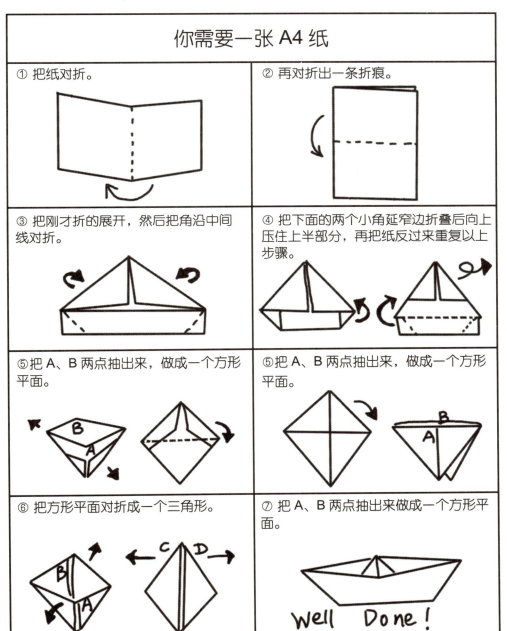

   nest

   nut

   nail

你能从下面的列车里找出熟悉的单词吗？

munarrowstneedleoceannoisenoneoften

你能找到 nut 这个单词吗？你能找到几个单词？

f	a	s	t	n	u	m	b	e	r
a	n	o	n	e	a	n	d	e	s
c	a	c	e	n	a	i	l	e	t
e	r	e	w	u	m	a	i	q	e
n	r	a	s	t	o	b	g	u	t
e	o	n	a	e	n	y	h	a	t
s	w	o	i	e	g	z	t	l	l
t	e	t	l	t	o	x	i	o	e

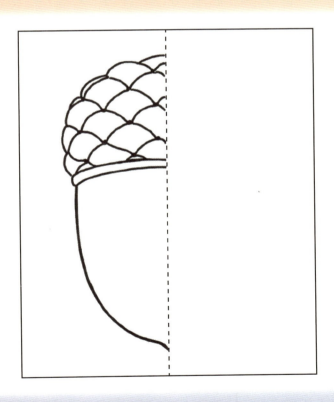

这是坚果吗？你能完成这个图片吗？上色看看？

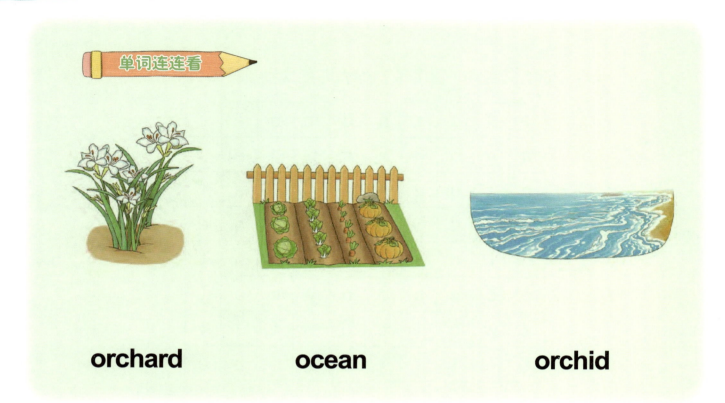

orchard   **ocean**   **orchid**

Own 的含义是

想设计一个你自己的蝴蝶吗？试试看。

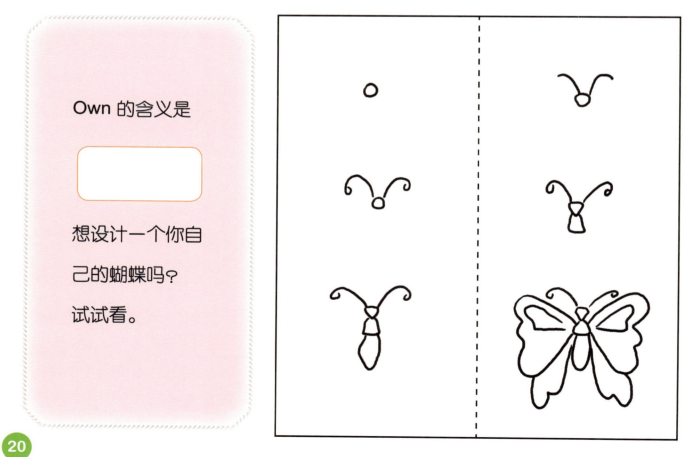

你能给这张图上色吗？

a	Red	f	Purple
b	Blue	g	Pink
c	Green	h	Orange
d	Yellow	i	Black
e	Brown	j	Gray

你能找到 party 这个单词吗？

你能找到几个单词？

p	l	e	a	s	e	i	n	t	o
l	l	o	p	l	e	n	t	y	o
e	a	j	a	n	g	r	y	o	u
n	t	u	r	o	l	l	a	p	n
t	e	n	t	h	e	n	a	i	i
y	l	e	y	e	l	l	o	t	v
e	j	t	p	o	c	k	e	t	s
p	o	l	e	a	r	n	s	e	e

单词连连看

quick   **quiet**   **quarter**

q	a	t	q	u	i	c	k	q	r
u	s	e	q	u	a	c	k	u	a
e	g	g	u	a	s	k	s	i	d
s	a	y	i	j	u	n	e	t	i
t	e	a	e	s	w	a	c	e	o
i	y	j	t	f	a	t	h	e	r
o	z	q	u	a	r	t	e	r	w
n	e	s	q	u	a	r	t	e	r

你能找到 quiet 这个单词吗？你能找到几个单词？

这株植物哪部分是花,哪部分是茎,哪部分是叶,哪部分是根?能用不同的颜色区分出来吗?

花的单词是

茎的单词是

叶的单词是

根的单词是

 单词连连看

    rain   **repair**   **rainbow**

他们在做什么？他们在航行，航行的单词是 _____。你能给下图上色吗？按数字上色哦！

1	Gray
2	Black
3	Orange
4	Pink
5	Purple
6	Brown
7	Yellow
8	Green
9	Blue
10	Red

你能找到几个 spider？

哪个是陆龟？哪个是海龟？连连看。

 turtle

 tortoise

下面的单词列车里你能找到熟悉的单词吗？

retrueswingtouchstaytomorrowstoptrunkthin

单词连连看

town　　　　　thermometer　　　　theater

下图哪个是整洁的房间？哪个房间乱？你的房间是什么样的呢？

untidy

tidy

umbrella　　　　uniform　　　　use

我要去看望爷爷奶奶，用哪个词更合适？

I'm going to _____ my grandparents.

A: see

B: visit

C: look

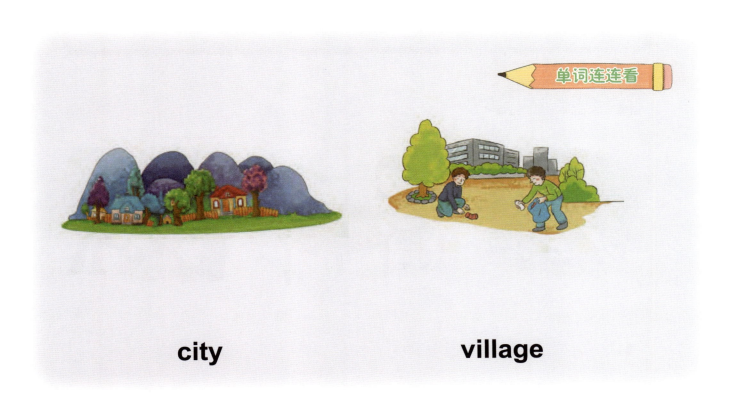

city　　　　　village

Wrong 和 Right

下面的图，哪个挂对了？哪个挂错了？连连看。

right　　　　　　　　wrong

单词连连看

work　　　　　　walk　　　　　　wipe

在下面的单词列车里,你能找到哪些熟悉的单词?

thinwearreadbewellrootwipethewin

这个男孩正在做什么?他在弹木琴。

木琴的单词是

yell   **yolk**   **yacht**

哦，今天太冷了，温度计已经降到了零度。这句话的英文少了一个单词，你能给补上吗？

Oh, how cold today! The thermometer fell to _____ .

你能给下面的图上色吗？

动手动脑趣味多
英语越学越快乐

使用说明

① 学完一部分做相应的练习，以达到复习巩固的目的。

② 家长为孩子念题，引导孩子自主完成。

③ 孩子练习时家长给予鼓励，孩子完成后要及时评价、表扬。

WORDS for ESL LEARNERS

情景英语4000词

4 常用动词

1000词

练习册
ACTIVITY BOOK

3～8岁

北京大学出版社
PEKING UNIVERSITY PRESS

下图表达了两种不同的态度。

Accept 的含义是 _____。Refuse 的含义是 _____。

你能为下图配上合适的英文单词吗?

Aa

单词连连看

   act

   appear

   aim

你在学校上台表演过吗？唱歌？跳舞？还是演奏乐器？

"这个小女孩喜欢表演。"这句话用英文怎么说？你知道吗？

水烧开了，水沸腾了。现在你知道这个词是什么了，对，就是 boil。
你能看图给下面的句子填空吗？

Is the kettle [_____] ?

在下面的单词列车里，你能找到哪些熟悉的单词？

adbumpcallbreatheoffbuygobiteadd

build　　　**barbecue**　　　**brush**

这个男孩正在做什么呢?

他在吹气球,你能给下面的句子填空吗?

The little boy ⬚ a balloon.

你能找到 come 吗？你能找到几个单词？这些单词里哪些是动词？

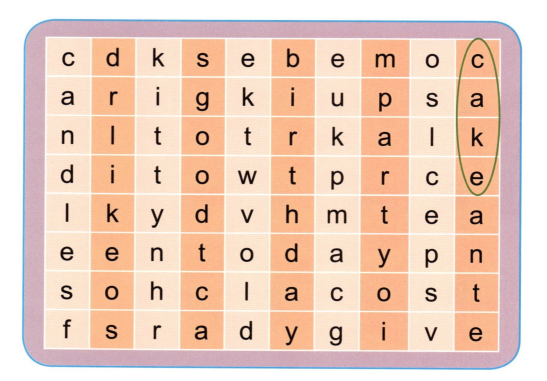

九月到来了，树上的叶子怎么了？看图给下面的句子填空。

September had _____ and the

leaves were starting to fall.

单词连连看

clean

cluck

carve

你能从下面的列车里找出熟悉的单词吗?

thcleanonclearblowcatchjumcheckram

Draw 的中文含义是什么？你知道吗？画一只小狗试试。

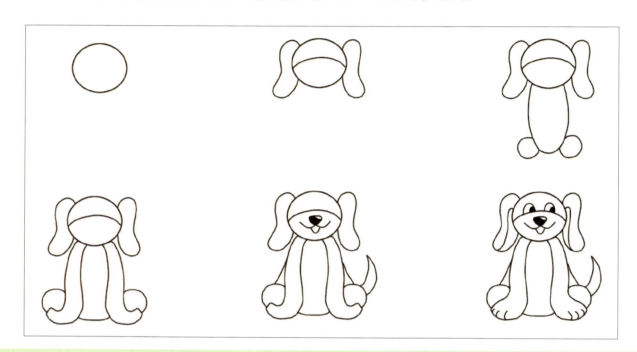

单词连连看

decorate   **drill**   **dance**

你看，这个皇帝总喜欢穿漂亮的衣服。

你能看图给下面的句子填空吗？

There was an emperor who liked to ⬜ in fine clothes.

花蝴蝶正在做什么？噢，它要吃花蜜。里面还有什么小动物？上色后看看，好看吗？

单词连连看

enter　　　　　　**eat**　　　　　　**earn**

小男孩不会拼写单词，怎么办？老师解释给她听。

下面这句话的英文少了一个单词，你知道是什么吗？

The teacher is _____ to the boy how to spell.

Could you help the mama bird find her babies?

你能帮助鸟妈妈找到它的宝宝吗？

这个人在做什么？

哦，他在钓鱼。

钓鱼的单词是 _____

这条鱼怎么啦？

哦，它害怕得跳了起来！

你能给图上色吗？

Gg

单词连连看

     glow   grill   glide

Garden 和 Garden

下面两个英文句子里的"garden"是相同的含义吗？是不同的吗？为什么？有什么不同？

This is my little garden.

这是我的小花园。

Gardening is my hobby.

在花园种植东西是我的爱好。

下图的孩子抱着妈妈,他为什么这样做呢?他感谢妈妈,对吗?

试着上色吧,不同的字母代表不同的颜色,这样好看吗?

或许你有自己的想法,试试看。

| a-Red | c-Green | e-Brown | g-Pink | i-Black |
| k-Gray | r-Orange | x-Purple | y-Yellow | z-Blue |

单词连连看

heat   **hose**   **head**

他在做什么呢？噢，他在熨衣服。你帮妈妈熨过衣服吗？

Can you iron a shirt?

这句话的中文含义是什么呢？

单词连连看

injure   invent   increase

你想象过自己像鸟一样飞吗？大声用英语说出自己的想法吧！

I ⬚ myself flying like a bird.

这个女孩正在做什么呢？噢，她在慢跑。

你也慢跑锻炼身体吗？

She is jogging in the park.

这句话的中文含义是什么呢？

单词连连看

jack up　　　**jingle**　　　**jump up**

He jacked up the car and changed the tire.

这句话是什么意思？你知道吗？

书里有哦！

毒品的危害非常大。

我们要远离毒品。

I keep off drugs.

这句话你记住了吗?

单词连连看

kneel　　　**kiss**　　　**knit**

你能找到几个 kitty?

k	i	y	t	k	i	t
i	i	t	y	i	y	y
t	y	t	k	t	i	t
t	k	i	t	t	y	t
y	t	k	i	y	i	i
y	t	t	i	k	t	k

单词连连看

ladle　　　　**light**　　　　**land**

想一想，你和好朋友在一起喜欢做什么呢？你们为什么是好朋友？试着完成下面的句子。比如：My friends and I like to play football.

My friends and I like to eat _____.

My friends and I like to read _____.

My friends and I like to watch _____.

I like my friends because _____.

My friends like me because _____.

不会的单词可以查词典哦！

邀请你的好朋友一起给图上色，可以按提示的数字上色，也可以按自己的想法上色哦，哪种好看？

Mm

单词连连看

    mince   mow   mend

Milk 和 Milk

下面两个句子中的"milk"含义是一样的吗？有区别吗？区别是什么？

She is milking a cow.

她正在挤牛奶。

The girl drank up that bottle of milk.

这个女孩喝光了瓶里的牛奶。

两个小朋友找他们的猫，他们找到了吗？

是的，他们听到小猫咪咪叫，咪咪叫的单词是

☐ 。

nip   **nail**   **nurse**

Name 和 Name

下面两句中的 name 含义是一样的吗？有区别吗？区别是什么？

We named our baby Jane.

我们给宝宝起名为简。

My name is Jack.

我的名字是杰克。

爸爸下班回来，他累了，坐在沙发上打盹。

你能给下面的句子填空吗？

He's ⬚ in the couch.

你和爸爸妈妈去餐厅吃饭的时候，你点菜吗？

你点你爱吃的菜吗？

图里的小女孩很棒，她说：

I can order food in a restaurant in English.

这句话的中文含义是什么？

如果不知道，可以查书哦！

单词连连看

overturn　　　　　obey　　　　　open

想到 order 这个单词，你还能想起哪些趣事？

把这些趣事对应的英文单词填入下面的摩天轮里吧，中文也可以哦！

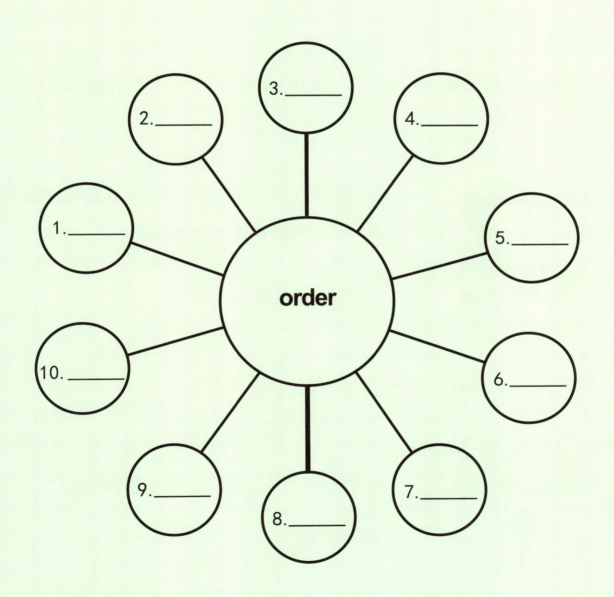

 单词连连看

parachute　　　　**pump**　　　　**pedal**

这个男孩对他的狗狗很好，他总是轻轻地拍它。

The child gently patted the dog on the head.

这句话的中文含义是什么？

书里有哦。

这几个女孩做什么呢？她们照相，每个人都摆了一个姿势。你知道这个英文单词是什么吗？

我知道，是 ☐ 。

Qq

单词连连看

quack　　　　**queue up**　　　　**quarter**

你能给下面的图上色吗？按提示的数字上色，效果怎么样？

1-Gray	2-Black
3-Orange	4-Pink
5-Purple	6-Brown
7-Yellow	8-Green
9-Blue	10-Red

Rr

roast   ride   race

你能写出下面和天气相关的单词吗？可以查词典哦！

ra__n   __lo__d

w__nd   s__n

__liz__ard   sn__wf__ake

t__rn__do   t__ermome__er

lig__tn__ng   __ain__ow

你认为小老鼠会与猫咪分享它的奶酪吗？你的回答是什么？为什么？
给这幅图上色吧，给你的好朋友也看看吧。

1	Gray
2	Black
3	Orange
4	Pink
5	Purple
6	Brown
7	Yellow
8	Green
9	Blue
10	Red

你知道"打喷嚏"这个词怎么说吗？对了，是 sneeze。

不过，你知道应该怎样打喷嚏比较合适吗？尤其人多的时候。下面的句子你有印象吗？书里有哦！

The boy should put his hands over his mouth when he sneezes.

这个男孩打喷嚏的时候应该捂住嘴。

单词连连看

      sow   smile   snow

Turn on 和 Turn off

Turn on 和 Turn off 的中文含义是什么？它们有区别吗？区别是什么？

用这两个词给下面的句子填空，如果不会可以翻书看看哦！

Would you mind ☐ the radio?

这句话的中文含义是什么？

It's so dark. Someone has ☐ the light.

这句话的中文含义是什么？

Uu

单词连连看

    unset   **underline**   **unroll**

鲍勃往车上装满了货物，然后鲍勃又卸下货物。用哪两个词表达这两个含义呢？"load"还是"unload"？说一说。

你在家里经常帮妈妈干家务吗?

"用吸尘器清理沙发上的面包屑。"

这句话你会用英语说吗?

单词连连看

vacuum　　　　　　　　　　vanish

这两个小孩正在做什么？

他们正在挥手。

挥手的英文单词是

给这幅图上色，

分享给你的好朋友看看。

 单词连连看

wash　　　　　**wrap**　　　　　**watch**

填空。先不要翻书哦！

如果不会写，再翻书哦！

We saw people _____ for help.

这句话的中文含义是什么？

单词连连看

yell　　　　　　　　yawn

zoom **zip**

动物园的单词是 ☐ 。想到动物园，你还能想到哪些有关的词？

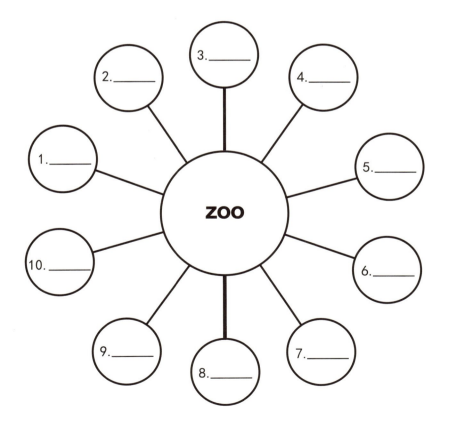

动手动脑趣味多
英语越学越快乐

使用说明

1. 学完一部分做相应的练习，以达到复习巩固的目的。
2. 家长为孩子念题，引导孩子自主完成。
3. 孩子练习时家长给予鼓励，孩子完成后要及时评价、表扬。

每天5分钟，单词积累不用愁

3～8岁

WORDS for ESL LEARNERS
情景英语4000词

③ 常用字典 1000词

沧浪文化英语创研室 ◎ 编著　戴维·帕特里克·泰奇　王威 ◎ 审订

北京大学出版社
PEKING UNIVERSITY PRESS

使用说明

为中国孩子量身定制的图画字典

纯正美音配音，给孩子最佳语感

学习单词　用扫描二维码、下载MP3文件或点读的方式学习单词的正确发音。听、读例句，了解此单词的正确用法。

复习单词　孩子对单词比较熟悉以后，家长可以和孩子玩"请你说一说"的游戏，如妈妈说中文，孩子说英语并找出书中对应的图画。以此熟悉单词，并提升观察力。

内容介绍

图画生动，例句权威，积累词汇量，效果100分！

→ **Word 单词**
按字母顺序排列，字大突出，一目了然。

→ **Translation 单词翻译**
准确的中文翻译，帮助孩子理解词义。

→ **Translation 句子翻译**
用"美语之路"点读笔点 译，即可听到中文翻译。

→ **Illustration 插图**
生动的插图，吸引孩子注意力并帮助理解、加深记忆。

→ **Example Sentence 例句**
每个单词都配有标准例句，帮助孩子准确掌握。

音频收听说明

朗读 贝蒂娜·朱莉

美国哥伦比亚大学表演系研究生,为"美语之路"系列图书配音,语音纯正,音质清晰。

语音评测

① **扫码** 扫描封底的二维码,关注微信公众号。

② **语音测评** 选择测评内容,开始录音,会有测评分数打出。

扫描二维码

① **扫码** 扫描封底的二维码,关注"沧浪文化"公众号。

② **听音频** 点击公众号右下角的"微课和音频",选择收听本书音频。

下载 MP3 文件

① **进入官网** 百度搜索"沧浪文化书馨网"。

② **下载** 点击首页右上角的"下载专区",下载本书 MP3 文件。

点读

● 本书支持:"小达人"和"美语之路"点读笔(需另购)。
● 正文中的文字和图片都可以点读。

① 打开电源开关　　② 点击封面　　③ 点读正文中的学习内容

目录 Contents

- 2 A a
- 5 B b
- 7 C c
- 12 D d

- 14 E e
- 16 F f
- 17 G g
- 19 H h

- 22 I i
- 23 J j
- 23 K k
- 24 L l

- 26 M m
- 29 N n
- 31 O o
- 33 P p

- 36 Q q
- 37 R r
- 39 S s
- 48 T t

- 53 U u
- 54 V v
- 55 W w
- 59 X x
- 59 Y y
- 59 Z z

Aa

accident 意外
He was injured in an **accident** at work. 译

afraid 害怕
I'm **afraid** of water. 译

again 又，再
Let's turn left and then turn left **again**. 译

against 倚，靠
She leaned **against** him. 译

age 年龄
The number of candles is the person's **age**. 译

allow 允许
Father will **allow** me to go. 译

alike 相似的
The two cars are much **alike**. 译

alive 活的
It feels great to be **alive**. 译

all 全部的
She works **all** year round. 译

alone 一个人
I want to travel **alone**. 译

along 沿着，顺着
Go **along** the new street. 译

also 也
She **also** likes playing the piano. 译

always 总是
You **always** do your homework well. 译

am 是（主语是"我"）
I **am** Millie from Class 1, Grade 7. 译

among 当中
Among all my subjects, I like English. 译

and 和
She **and** I are students. 译

angry 生气的
The king was very **angry** and shouted, "Go away!" 译

any 任何
Sorry, I don't have **any** cake. 译

anyone 任何人
He will not tell **anyone**. 译

anything 任何东西
Tom does not want to eat **anything**. 译

are 是（主语是"他们／她们／它们"）
They **are** teachers. 译

argue 争论
He's always willing to **argue** for what is right. 译

army 军队
My cousin served in the **army**. 译

around 在……周围
The children sit **around** their mother.

arrive 到达
Don't **arrive** late for class.

arrow 箭，箭头
The **arrow** on the map points north.

artist 画家
My aunt is an **artist**.

asleep 睡着
He fell **asleep** at around 3:00 a.m..

assembly 聚会
They will attend the **assembly**.

astronaut 宇航员
I want to be an **astronaut**.

at 在
I stand **at** her right.

attention 注意力
You must pay **attention** to the traffic lights.

awake 醒来
It is midday when lions **awake**.

away 离开
The rubbish should be carted **away** at once.

Bb

bad 坏的，严重的
I have a **bad** headache. 译

badge 徽章
The boy pins a **badge** on to his jacket. 译

bang 巨响，砰
A sudden **bang** made the cat jump. 译

bank 银行
Where's the **bank**? It's next to the post office. 译

balcony 阳台
Keep the dogs on the **balcony**. 译

bean sprout 豆芽
I like eating **bean sprouts**. 译

beetle 甲虫
A firefly is a type of **beetle**. 译

beak 鸟嘴
The bird opened its **beak** and sang. 译

beautiful 美丽的
You have the most **beautiful** smile. 译

bell 铃，钟
We heard the church **bells** ringing. 译

belong 属于
The hair band might **belong** to Linda. 译

below 下面
He dived **below** the surface of the water. 译

5

bench 长椅
My mother is sitting on a **bench** now. 译

beside 旁边
There is a table **beside** the bed. 译

blank 空白
Fill in the **blank**. 译

blind 盲的
He is **blind**. 译

both 两者，都
They **both** love riding. 译

bottle 瓶子
I lost my **bottle**. 译

bottom 底
He sat at the **bottom** of the stairs. 译

bow 蝴蝶结
There is a **bow** on the gift box. 译

bow 鞠躬
Bow before the king. 译

breakfast 早餐
It's time for **breakfast**. 译

breath 呼吸
It's so cold outside that I can see my **breath**. 译

bring 拿，带
They **brought** lunch to the park. 译

bucket 桶
It's a large **bucket** of flowers.

buffalo 水牛
This **buffalo** looks angry.

busy 忙碌的
Farmers are **busy** in autumn.

but 但是
Linda is short, **but** she's good at basketball.

butcher 肉贩
My uncle is a **butcher**.

by 旁边
His wife was sitting **by** his side.

Cc

cage 笼子
There is a monkey in the **cage**.

calendar 日历
I need a desk **calendar** for my new term.

call 叫
The birds are **calling** as the sun rises.

camp 露营
I **camped** in the mountain with my family.

can 会，能
I **can** take care of my sister.

canary 金丝雀
The **canary** in the cage is yellow.

candle 蜡烛
There are five **candles** in her birthday cake.

canteen 食堂
I often go to the school **canteen** for lunch.

careful 小心
Be **careful**! The stove is hot!

careless 粗心的
Careless people always forget to turn off the power.

carpenter 木匠
The **carpenter** works day and night.

car 车，车厢
There is a dining **car** on the train.

cartoon 卡通片
John wants to watch **cartoons**.

caterpillar 毛毛虫
The girl is afraid of **caterpillars**.

cave 山洞
They hid in a **cave**.

ceiling 天花板
The **ceiling** is low in the room.

cent 一分钱
We haven't got a **cent**.

center 中心
The paper is white with a large red circle in the **center**. 译

change 换
Change the television channel, please. 译

cheek 面颊
Kiss your mother on the **cheek**. 译

child 儿童
The **child** often watches TV in the evening. 译

chilli 辣椒
The **chilli** makes my eyes full of tears. 译

chocolate 巧克力
Do you want some **chocolate**? 译

choose 选择
Which shirt would you **choose**? 译

chop 砍,劈
No **chopping**! 译

city 城市
We should make our **city** clean. 译

clap 鼓掌
If you are happy, **clap** your hands. 译

class 班,课
I use pencils in art **class**. 译

cleaner 吸尘器
I can't get the **cleaner** under these chairs. 译

clever 聪明的
She's **clever** and pretty. 译

climb 爬
We **climbed** up the hill. 译

clinic 诊所
You can wait outside the **clinic**. 译

close 关
Close the door, please. 译

coast 海岸，海边
He lives on the **coast**. 译

cobra 眼镜蛇
The **cobra** bit him. 译

cobweb 蜘蛛网
The barn is filled with **cobwebs**. 译

coconut 椰子
Coconut milk has little nutritious value. 译

coffee 咖啡
Would you like some **coffee** or tea? 译

coin 硬币
Here are some gold **coins**. 译

cold 冷的，感冒
John had a **cold**. 译

collect 拾，收集
They are **collecting** water. 译

compare 比较

I **compared** several bicycles before buying one. 译

corner 角落

I found a little boy crying in the **corner**. 译

count 数一数

To **count** from 1 to 10. 译

cowboy 牧牛者，牛仔

He is an American **cowboy**. 译

crab 螃蟹

The **crab** can't jump. 译

cone 圆锥

The child is licking his ice cream **cone**. 译

correct 正确的

The **correct** answers can be found at the bottom of page 8. 译

country 国家

The food in the **country** is nice and cheap. 译

crane 起重机

She can operate a **crane**. 译

cook 厨师，烹饪

Cook for five minutes and add two eggs. 译

cot 婴儿床

He climbed out of his **cot**. 译

cow 牛

She is milking a **cow**. 译

crash 哗啦一声，撞到

The car **crashed** into another. 译

crayon 蜡笔

How many **crayons** do you have? 译

croak 呱呱叫

We could hear a frog **croaking** in the pond. 译

crooked 弯曲的，歪的

The picture hangs **crooked**. 译

cross 穿过

Some elephants are **crossing** the road. 译

crow 乌鸦

Don't make a loud noise like a **crow**. 译

crowd 众人

She loves singing in front of **crowds**. 译

cry 哭

The woman is **crying**. 译

cucumber 黄瓜

Cucumber is long and green. 译

curry 咖喱

The Indian boy enjoys **curry**. 译

Dd

danger 危险

Giant pandas are now in **danger** of becoming extinct. 译

dark 黑暗的

Don't read in the **dark**. It's bad for your eyes. 译

date 日期

We don't know the **date** of his birth. 译

day 白天
He works all **day**.

dead 死的
The **dead** tree fell down.

deaf 聋的
My grandfather is **deaf**.

deep 深的
The water is **deep** in the middle of the lake.

different 不同的
Chinese food is so **different** from British ones.

dining room 餐厅
Let's take the dishes into the **dining room**.

dinner 晚餐
We have **dinner** at 7:00 in the evening.

dirty 肮脏的
Don't leave the **dirty** dishes in the kitchen.

dollar 美元
She gave me one dollar.

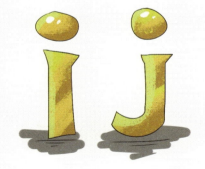

dot 点
There are **dots** above the letters i and j.

down 下去
Jump up and **down** ten times.

downstairs 下楼
Denise went **downstairs** and made some tea.

dragonfly 蜻蜓
We often see **dragonflies** in summer.

drain 沟渠，下水道
They had to unblock the **drain**.

dream 做梦
I **dreamt** of dinosaurs. They were running after me!

dust 灰尘
The floor was covered with **dust**.

duster 板擦
Could you hand me the **duster**?

during 在……期间
During the weekend, Ding usually gets up at 8:00 a.m..

dwarf 矮人
The naughty boy laughed at the **dwarf**.

Ee

each 每个
Each student can draw a picture.

eagle 鹰
The **eagle** has good eyesight.

early 早的
Does she get up **early**?

earth 地球
Everyone should play a role in saving the **earth**.

earthquake 地震
The town was destroyed by an **earthquake**.

electricity 电力
The clock hasn't been working since the **electricity** was off. 译

elf 小精灵
The **elf** is like a child. 译

empty 空的，清空
Could you help me **empty** the trash? 译

engine 引擎
My car had to have a new **engine**. 译

enjoy 喜欢
Meimei **enjoys** reading. 译

enough 足够
She asked for **enough** money from her mother. 译

entrance 入口
We took photos in front of the **entrance**. 译

equal 相同的
Tom is **equal** to Mary in height. 译

eraser 橡皮
The **eraser** is next to the pen and the ruler. 译

exercise 运动
I **exercise** three times a week. 译

estate 住宅区
She lives in a tower block on an **estate** in New York. 译

every 每一个
I plan to go swimming **every** week. 译

exit 出口
Let's turn off the motorway at **exit** 9. 译

15

Ff

factory 工厂
Miss Bird is a **factory** worker.

fall 落下，秋天
The leaves **fall** and **fall**. I love **fall**.

fat 胖的
Look at the cat. It is **fat**.

fence 围墙，围栏
We put up a **fence** around our yard.

fern 蕨类植物
There are many kinds of **fern** in the jungle.

field 田野
Cows were grazing in the **field**.

fierce 凶恶的
Their dog was so **fierce** that no one dared to come near it.

fight 打架
Don't **fight**.

film 电影
I love the **film**.

fingernail 指甲
He had dirt under his **fingernails**.

flat 公寓
Well, there're different websites you can go on to find a **flat**.

flood 水灾，洪水
The water has risen to **flood** level.

floor 地上
Jack is sitting on the **floor** and watching TV.

fly 飞
The wild geese **fly** from north to south.

forest 森林
There is a house in the **forest**.

forget 忘记
Don't **forget** to say "good morning"!

for 为了
I have ordered lunch **for** you.

full 满的
The glass is **full** of water.

fun 乐趣，有趣的
Painting is **fun**.

fur 软毛，毛皮
Rabbit has soft **fur**.

form 形成，排成
They **formed** a circle and sang a song.

Gg

furniture 家具
He is dusting the **furniture**.

garage 车库
There is a **garage** in the house.

garden 花园
Go into the **garden** and water the flowers.

17

gardener 园丁
My grandfather is a **gardener**.

gas 煤气
Coal is actually cheaper than **gas**.

ghost 鬼
Three **ghosts** visit Scrooge that night.

giant 巨人
Have you read the story "The Selfish **Giant**"?

give 给
What does Helen want to **give** her grandma?

glass 玻璃
There is a large **glass** window in front of the house.

gold 黄金
The emperor had to send them silk and **gold**.

good 好的
I'm **good** at maths.

goodbye 再见
We will say **goodbye** to each other.

grasshopper 蚱蜢
The **grasshopper** said: " I am singing all summer long."

great 大的
There is a **great** quantity of fish over there.

greedy 贪心的，渴望的
The children were **greedy** for more candies.

grocer 杂货店
I buy fruits and vegetables in the **grocer**. 译

ground 地上
Peter kept his eyes on the **ground**. 译

group 群，组
She joined a discussion **group**. 译

grow 生长
Look! How well the crops **grow**! 译

guinea pig 豚鼠
Two **guinea pigs** crawled toward the cave. 译

gun 枪
I go out with my **gun** almost every day to hunt animals for food. 译

Hh

half 一半
We got up at **half** past eight. 译

hammer 锤子
The clerk gave him a **hammer**. 译

handkerchief 手帕
He took out a **handkerchief**. 译

handsome 英俊的
He is really **handsome**. 译

hang 挂
I'll **hang** up the decorations. 译

harbour 港口

The **harbour** admits large tankers and freighters. 译

hard 硬的

The baby can't eat the **hard** cheese. 译

hard-working 勤奋的

She's quiet and very **hard-working**. 译

hat 帽子

— Where's my **hat**?
— It's on your head! 译

headmaster 校长

The **headmaster** is not in the office. 译

hawk 鹰

He told us a story about a **hawk**. 译

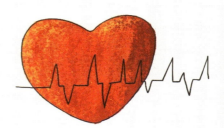

headmistress 女校长

The **headmistress** was an Oxford graduate. 译

heart 心

I felt nervous and my **heart** was beating fast. 译

heavy 重的

My schoolbag is **heavy**. 译

height 高度

His **height** is 1.64 metres. 译

hello 你好

Hello! How are you? 译

help 帮助
Some passengers **helped** to get the old man onto the bus.

here 这里
I wondered how he came **here**.

hit 击打
Someone got **hit** on the head.

holiday 假期
What did you do for the **holiday**?

home 家
It's time to go **home**, kids.

hook 钩子
Hang your towel on the **hook**.

hot 热的
Summer is **hot** and the days are long.

hotel 酒店
He takes the No. 17 bus to a **hotel**.

hour 小时
There are 60 minutes in an **hour**.

how 怎样，如何
How do I get to your home?

hungry 饿
They were **hungry** because they hadn't had lunch.

hurt 伤，受伤
He always **hurts** himself.

Ii

ill 生病的
Mum, I feel **ill**.

insect 昆虫
He found ants and other **insects**.

invite 邀请
We are happy to **invite** you to a farewell party.

is 是
The best thing to do **is** smile.

ice 冰
Can I have some **ice** cream, please?

in 在……里
I like to swim **in** the sea.

inside 里面
I went **inside** the building.

island 岛
The **island** is covered with trees.

idea 主意
Good **idea**!

into 进入
Turn left **into** Park Road.

iron 熨斗，熨平
Mother is **ironing** out the wrinkles.

it 它
I have looked **it** up in a dictionary.

Jj

Jeep 越野车
He came out of the **Jeep**.

jelly 果冻
I love **jellies** and jams.

jellyfish 水母
Most **jellyfish** have no eyes.

jetty 码头
This **jetty** has been destroyed by the waves.

join 参加
Let's **join** the basketball club!

joke 笑话
You can learn some great **jokes**.

jungle 丛林
There are many **jungles** in the tropical areas.

Kk

kangaroo 袋鼠
You can see **kangaroos** in Australia.

keep 保持
I asked them to **keep** quiet.

kettle 水壶
The **kettle** is boiling.

kind 善良的
She's very **kind**, but she's strict sometimes.

king 国王
Mike was singing for the **king**.

knock 敲
He **knocked** at the door. 译

knot 结
She tied the rope in a **knot**. 译

know 知道，懂得
Do you **know** his address? 译

Ll

labourer 工人
Her husband is a farm **labourer**. 译

ladle 长柄勺子，用勺子舀起
The soup was **ladled** into the bowls. 译

land 陆地，降落
A spaceship was trying to **land** on an unknown planet. 译

lantern 灯笼
The child next door carried a **lantern**. 译

lap 腿上
A child is sitting on his **lap**. 译

large 大的
The main dish is almost always turkey, a **large** bird. 译

last 最后
My horse was the **last** in the race. 译

late 迟到
It's eight o'clock. Oh dear! I'm **late** for school. 译

laugh 笑
The audience was **laughing** loudly. 译

lazy 懒惰的
I was too **lazy** to go running. 译

learn 学
Today we'll **learn** some kung fu. 译

left 左
Turn **left** at the bookstore. 译

length 长度
What is the **length** of the pencil? 译

less 少
Eat **less** sugar. 译

lesson 课
She's been taking piano **lessons** for years. 译

light 灯，轻的
Wait! Don't go at the red **light**! 译

lift 电梯，提升
We have to walk up because there is no **lift**. 译

like 喜欢
My brother **likes** baseball. 译

litter 垃圾
The sign means you can't **litter** here. 译

lightning 闪电
Since it starts **lightning**, we'd better go inside. 译

line 线
The ball went over the **line**. 译

lily 百合
She holds **lilies** in her hands. 译

little 小的
What's the **little** monkey doing? 译

lobster 龙虾
Someone is allergic to **lobster**.

lock 锁
There is a **lock** in the door.

long 长
The giraffe has a **long** neck.

lorry 货车
The goods will be carried by **lorry** to the factory.

lose 丢失
She **lost** her bag.

loud 大声的
He is singing in a **loud** voice.

love 爱
I **love** you.

low 低
The sun is getting **lower** and **lower**.

lunch 午餐
It's time for **lunch**. Let's have some chicken.

Mm

magic 魔术，魔法的
The Monkey King uses a **magic** stick.

magician 魔术师
He is an excellent **magician**.

26

make 做
Can I **make** a snowman? 译

man 男人
He was a shy boy, but he grew to be a strong and confident **man**. 译

mandarin 柑橘
This is a **mandarin**. 译

mangosteen 山竹
The **mangosteen** has a gorgeous, thick, purple rind. 译

mango 芒果
Do you like eating **mangos**? 译

market 市场
There is a big **market** near my home. 译

match 比赛，火柴
I am watching a football **match** on TV. 译

many 多少
How **many** English classes do they have a week? 译

measure 测量
Measure the length and width of the gap. 译

meat 肉
Some dinosaurs ate **meat**. 译

may 可以
You **may** chalk it on the wall. 译

medicine 药
He knows a lot about Chinese **medicine**. 译

meet 遇见
Let's **meet** this Saturday. 译

metre 米
His height is 1.64 **metres**.

middle 中间
He was standing in the **middle** of the room.

mine 我的
Your feet are bigger than **mine**.

minute 分钟
Don't worry. I can do it in a **minute**.

miss 想念，错过
He **misses** his family and the delicious food made by his mother.

mix 配料，混合
Next, fill the turkey with this bread **mix**.

more 更多的
He spent **more** time studying.

morning 早上
It is Saturday **morning** now.

mosquito 蚊子
There is a **mosquito** bite on my arm.

most 最多的
The man with the **most** beautiful flowers can have the bonus!

move 搬，移动
I just **moved** into an old house.

much 多少
How **much** is this T-shirt?

mud 泥浆
He is stuck in the **mud**.

mug 大杯
He drank a **mug** of coffee.

muscle 肌肉
She started lifting weights to build **muscle**.

museum 博物馆
Where is the science **museum**?

music 音乐
They have **music** class on Tuesday and Friday.

must 必须
You **must** not smoke in the classroom.

Nn

my 我的
Welcome to **my** home.

nail 钉子
The worker needs some **nails**.

name 名字
My **name** is Amy.

narrow 窄的
The city's ancient streets are too **narrow** for buses.

naughty 淘气的
He's just too **naughty**.

near 接近,旁边

Where is the kite? It is **near** the windows. 译

necktie 领带

Which **necktie** is your favourite? 译

needle 针,指针

The compass **needle** points north. 译

neighbour 邻居

We invited our friends and **neighbours**. 译

nest 巢

The bird built a **nest** out of small twigs. 译

never 从不

Jane **never** washes her socks herself. 译

new 新的

We have a **new** classroom. 译

news 新闻

I have some good **news** and some bad **news**. 译

newspaper 报纸

I'm going to write articles for magazines and **newspapers**. 译

next 在……旁边

The art room is **next** to the gym. 译

night 晚上

He sleeps all **night** and works all day. 译

nobody 没有人

There is **nobody** in the room. 译

noise 声音

The dogs made a **noise**, a rough, grumbling sound. 译

none 没有

"Is there any more milk?" "No, **none** at all." 译

noodle 面条

I'd like to have some **noodles**. It's my birthday today. 译

nothing 没有东西

There's **nothing** in my hands. 译

number 号码

What is his phone **number**? 译

nut 坚果

Crack a **nut**. 译

Oo

ocean 海洋

No ocean in the world is as big as the Pacific **Ocean**. 译

octopus 章鱼

Japanese love eating **octopus**. 译

office 办公室

The teachers' **office** is next to the library. 译

officer 官员，军官

He is an **officer** of the court. 译

often 经常

He **often** has lunch with his father. 译

oil 油
My father added a little **oil** into the pan. 译

old 旧的，古老的
These books are very **old**. 译

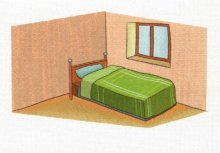

only 只有，唯一的
There is **only** one bed in the room. 译

opposite 在……对面
There was a big tree **opposite** the school. 译

or 或
Would you like beer, wine, **or** something else? 译

orchard 果园
There are many kinds of fruits in the **orchard**. 译

orchestra 管弦乐队
He plays violin in the school **orchestra**. 译

orchid 兰花
Those **orchids** are white. 译

out 出来
That chick pecks **out** an earthworm from the earth. 译

outside 外面
It's cold **outside**. 译

owl 猫头鹰
The **owl** is flying into the sky. 译

own 自己的
Susan has her **own** room. 译

Pp

page 页
Please turn to **page** ten.

pain 痛
She felt a sharp **pain** in her foot.

paint 油漆
They saw some large letters in white **paint**.

pair 双
Linda buys a **pair** of shoes for her mother.

palm 手掌
He placed a coin in the **palm** of the child.

papaya 木瓜
The **papaya** is good for our health.

parachute 降落伞
The pilot was wearing a **parachute**.

park 公园，停泊
I live near the **park**.

parrot 鹦鹉
The **parrot** is so smart.

part 部分
Part of the building was destroyed in the fire.

party 派对
We're having a **party** at school.

33

pattern 图案，纸样

The floral **pattern** on the dish is beautiful. 译

pavement 人行道

You can wait on the **pavement** look out for cars and bikes. 译

picnic 野餐

We sometimes have a **picnic** on the weekends. 译

pineapple 菠萝

There is a can of chopped **pineapple**. 译

plant 种植，植物

The old man has **planted** about 1,000 trees this year. 译

penguin 企鹅

Let's go to the polar museum to see the **penguins**. 译

petal 花瓣

The boy counted the **petals** one by one. 译

piece 块

Here is a **piece** of sweet cake. 译

pirate 海盗

Don't worry about the **pirates**. 译

person 人

I knew the **person** sitting here. 译

photograph 照片

I found this old **photograph** in the drawer. 译

pin 大头针，用针钉住

Pin the paper on the wall. 译

place 地方

There is an ancient building in this **place**. 译

plastic 塑料
The pipes may be made of **plastic**. 译

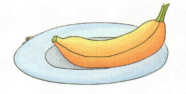

plate 盘子
There is a banana on the **plate**. 译

please 请
Please sit down. 译

plenty 很多
"Do we need more milk?" "No, there's **plenty** in the fridge." 译

pocket 口袋
He keeps his gloves in his **pocket**. 译

point 点
My pencil is sharp in the **point**. 译

pole 杆
He connected the **poles** of the tent. 译

pond 池塘
There is nothing but water in the **pond**. 译

pony 小马
I had a very good **pony**, called Brandy. 译

poor 穷的
They are **poor** paupers. 译

pork 猪肉
There is a packet of **pork** on the table. 译

port 港口
The ship reached the **port** safely. 译

prawn 虾
They all like eating **prawns**. 译

pray 祈祷
We **prayed** for their safe return. 译

pretty 美丽
She's **pretty** and clever.

prize 奖品
We will give **prizes** to our good students.

pupil 学生
The **pupils** hold many beautiful flowers in their hands.

puppet 木偶
The **puppet** looks very funny.

purse 钱包
Her **purse** is empty.

push 推
The hunter is **pushing** a big rock down the hill.

pajamas 睡衣裤
Take off your **pajamas**.

python 蟒
The **python** looks scary.

Qq

quarter 四分之一，一刻钟
It's a **quarter** past three in the afternoon.

question 问题
Can I ask a **question** about our maths homework?

quick 快的
The monkeys always move **quick**.

quiet 安静的
"Does she have to be **quiet** in the library?" "Yes."

quite 相当，很
There are **quite** a few photos here.

Rr

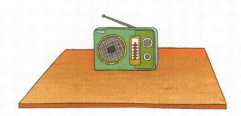

radio 收音机
My **radio** is on the desk.

rain 雨
It's **raining**.

rainbow 彩虹
Look! There is a **rainbow** over the river!

raincoat 雨衣
We forgot to bring our **raincoats**.

rash 皮疹
The baby has a **rash**.

rat 老鼠
The cat is good at catching **rats**.

rattle 拨浪鼓
The baby is waving her **rattle**.

raw 生的
This vegetable can be eaten **raw** or cooked.

ready 准备好
Are you **ready** for school?

real 真的
"Are those **real** snakes?" "No, they are toys."

recess 休息，课间休息
They all play together at **recess**.

rectangle 长方形
Draw a **rectangle** and a circle.

remember 记忆
I use a memory card to help me **remember** new words.

repair 修理
I can **repair** it.

reply 回复
We shall **reply** to this invitation early.

rest 其余，休息
We'd better **rest** after work.

ribbon 丝带
She wore pink **ribbons** in her hair.

rice 米
I'd like some **rice**, please.

rich 富有的
There's a **rich** old businessman in this small town.

right 右边的，对的
Keep to the **right**, please.

roar 轰鸣，吼
The thunder is **roaring** now. 译

roll 滚
The ball **rolled** slowly. 译

ring 响
The phone never stopped **ringing**. 译

roof 屋顶
The **roof** is leaking. 译

root 根
The potted plant has a shallow **root**. 译

rose 玫瑰
A red **rose** is on top of the cake. 译

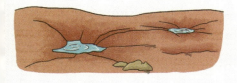

Ss

sack 袋子
The chicken pecked a hole in the **sack**. 译

rough 不平坦的
The ground is **rough**. 译

sad 悲伤的
The cat is ill. Sarah is **sad**. 译

safe 安全的
I will make it **safe**. 译

sail 帆
The sailors raised the **sails** of the ship. 译

39

salt 盐

Don't forget to add some **salt**. 译

same 一样的，相同的

Anna is the **same** age as me. 译

saw 锯子

This is a **saw**. 译

say 说

The girl **says** hello when she meets her teacher. 译

scare 惊吓，害怕

I was so **scared** that I couldn't move. 译

scarf 围巾

This **scarf** is for you. 译

scream 尖叫，大叫

The kids were **screaming** with excitement. 译

screw 螺丝

Tighten the **screws**. 译

seagull 海鸥

The teacher told us **seagulls** live near the ocean. 译

seat 座位

Comfortable **seats** are important for cinemas. 译

second 秒

It only takes forty **seconds**. 译

secret 秘密，秘密的

There is a **secret** passage behind the bookcase. 译

sell 卖

She **sold** her cows and pigs.

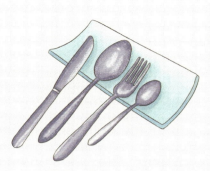

set 一套，摆放

A cutlery **set** includes a knife, a fork and spoons.

sew 缝

She **sews** her own dresses by hand.

shade 树荫，阴凉处

These plants grow well in **shade**.

shadow 影子

His **shadow** is getting longer and longer.

shallow 浅的

The river is so shallow.

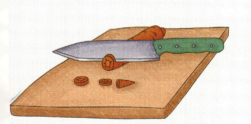

sharp 锋利的

This knife is very **sharp**.

sharpener 铅笔刀

I want to buy a **sharpener**.

she 她

She is my sister.

shell 壳

We collected **shells** at the beach.

shine 发光

When the moon is **shining** bright, we'll be able to see the stones.

ship 轮船

I'll go there by **ship**.

shoot 射
Hou Yi tried to **shoot** the Suns. 译

shop 商店
There are some small **shops** here. 译

shopkeeper 店主
The **shopkeeper** smiled towards us. 译

short 短的，矮的
She's **short** and thin. 译

shorts 短裤
Now I have a cool pair of **shorts** for riding. 译

shovel 铲
He is **shoveling** snow outside. 译

show 表演，演出
I love school **shows**. 译

shut 关闭，关闭的
He **shut** his eyes and fell asleep. 译

sick 有病的
He helps **sick** people. 译

side 旁边，一侧
In China, people drive on the right **side**. 译

signal 信号
The lighthouse flashes **signals** twice a minute. 译

sing 唱歌
She is **singing**. 译

sit 坐，位于
Two little birds are **sitting** on the wall.

sitting room 客厅
There are many flowers in the **sitting room**.

size 尺码
Can I try them on? **Size** 6, please.

skin 皮肤，皮
These snakes shed their **skins** once a year.

sky 天空
The **sky** is clear and the sun is bright.

sleep 睡觉
He is **sleeping**.

slice 片
They sell pizza by the **slice**.

slide 滑梯
The children run to the playground **slide**.

slide 滑动
The door **slides** easily.

slip 滑倒
You might **slip**!

slippery 滑的
The floor looks **slippery**.

smell 发出……的气味，气味
This fish **smells** bad.

smooth 平滑的

Silk feels **smooth** and soft.

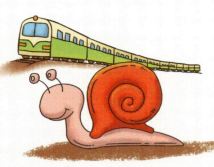

snail 蜗牛

The train is moving as slow as a **snail**.

snow 雪

"Which season do you like best?"
"Winter, because I like **snow**."

sock 袜子

My clothes and **socks** are in front of me.

soft 柔软的

This is a **soft** pillow.

soldier 士兵

When I grow up, I'll be a **soldier**.

some 一些

She picked **some** flowers in the garden.

sometimes 有时

We watch the evening news **sometimes**.

song 歌

Robin is singing a **song**.

sore 痛的

I have a **sore** back.

sound 声音

The erhu **sounded** so sad that I almost cried.

sorry 抱歉，遗憾

Oh, I'm **sorry** you fell ill. I'm glad you feel better now.

soup 汤
This **soup** is too cold.

sour 酸的
The lemon tastes **sour**.

space 空间，太空
There isn't much **space** for everybody.

spaceship 太空船
The **spaceship** is soaring into the sky.

spade 铲子
I dug with a **spade**.

spider 蜘蛛
A **spider** had spun a perfect web outside the window.

spinach 菠菜
The girl doesn't like **spinach**.

splash 泼，溅湿
The fountain is **splashing** out to the boy.

spot 斑点
There are many **spots** on the dog.

square 正方形的
This is a red **square** board.

squeeze 挤压，紧握
Mary is **squeezing** the juice from the orange.

squirrel 松鼠
Every day the **squirrels** have to give the Monkey King gifts.

stadium 体育场
The ceremony will be held in the **stadium**. 译

stamp 邮票
He has been collecting **stamps** since he was eight. 译

start 开始
We **start** at half past eight. 译

stay 停留
I will **stay** in Beijing for two days. 译

steal 偷
He is **stealing** a man's wallet. 译

steel 钢
The frame is made of **steel**. 译

still 静止的，平静的
The water is **still**. 译

step 步
The baby took her first **steps** today. 译

stick 粘贴
Stick a photo on the paper and then write about it. 译

stop 停
Slow down and **stop**! 译

stomach 胃
He places one hand on his **stomach**. 译

stomachache 肚子疼
I have a **stomachache**. 译

storm 暴风雨
What did you do during **storms**? 译

storeroom 储藏室
There is something useless in our **storeroom**.

story 故事
It's time for our **story**!

stove 炉子
She put the pan on the **stove**.

straight 直的
Do they have **straight** or curly hair?

string 绳子
She tied a **string** around the boxes.

stripe 条纹
Each white petal had a red **stripe**.

strong 强壮的
He grows to be a **strong** man.

submarine 潜水艇
The **submarine** can operate underwater.

subtract 减去
If we **subtract** 5 from 9, we get 4.

suck 吮吸
She is **sucking** on an orange slice.

sunburn 晒伤
He got **sunburn** in his face.

supper 晚餐
We are having **supper** now.

surprise 惊奇，惊讶的

"What happened?" she asked in **surprise**. 译

sweet 糖果

She often eats too many **sweets**. 译

swing 秋千，荡，挥舞

Sam is on the **swing**. 译

sword 剑

He is swinging his **sword**. 译

syrup 糖浆

It's better to mix milk with **syrup**. 译

Tt

T-shirt T恤衫

I wore a **T-shirt** and shorts. 译

tadpole 蝌蚪

I'm a little **tadpole**. I'm looking for mummy. 译

tail 尾巴

The fish has a big **tail**. 译

take 拿

Take this book to her, please. 译

tame 驯服的，温和的

The birds on the island are quite **tame**. 译

tank 坦克

The **tank** stopped. 译

48

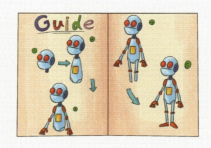

taste 品尝
Everything **tastes** good. 译

teach 教
The guide **teaches** us how to make a model robot. 译

tear 眼泪，撕破
She broke out in **tears**. 译

tell 告诉，讲述
The children are **telling** stories. 译

temperature 温度
The nurse took his **temperature**. 译

term 学期
I know how to plan my studies for the next **term**. 译

thank 多谢
"Happy birthday." "**Thank** you." 译

that 那，那个
That dress of hers is too short. 译

theater 剧院
We often go to the **theater** on weekends. 译

their 他们的/她们的/它们的
Lucy, what will you wear on **their** fashion show? 译

there 那里
Ask that girl over **there**. 译

they 他们/她们/它们
They are all laughing. 译

49

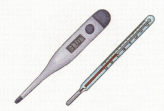

thermometer 体温计
These are **thermometers**. 译

thick 厚的
The mountains are covered with **thick** snow. 译

thief 小偷
The **thief** was arrested by the policeman. 译

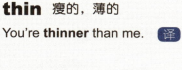

thin 瘦的，薄的
You're **thinner** than me. 译

think 想，认为
He's old but he **thinks** he's young. 译

thirsty 口渴的
She is hungry and **thirsty**. 译

thread 线
The girl is fixing the doll with needle and **thread**. 译

thorn 刺
Roses have **thorns**. 译

this 这
Is **this** your pencil? 译

through 穿过
The car is passing **through** Fifth Avenue. 译

throw 抛，扔
I'm not going to **throw** my doll away. 译

thumb 拇指
Hold out your **thumb** until a driver stops and gives you a lift. 译

thunder 雷
I heard a loud noise like **thunder**. 译

tick 钩
His exercise books were full of red **ticks**. 译

ticket 票
We can buy **tickets** quickly. 译

tidy 整齐的
The room is small but **tidy**. 译

time 时间
Do you know what **time** is it? 译

tin 罐
She bought a **tin** of soup. 译

tiny 小的
The **tiny** baby was crying all night. 译

tired 累的
You seem to be **tired**. 译

to 去
I'm going **to** clean my bedroom. 译

today 今天
What day is it **today**? 译

together 一起
At this festival, people get **together** with their families. 译

toilet 厕所
The child already knew how to use the **toilet**. 译

tomorrow 明天
I will go swimming **tomorrow**. 译

tonight 今晚
There'll be a heavy rain **tonight**. 译

tool 工具
I've brought back my **tools**. 译

top 顶
When we got to the **top**, it was raining hard. 译

torch 火炬，电筒
She says she's ready to pass the **torch**. 译

tortoise 陆龟
The **tortoise** moves slowly. 译

touch 摸
Don't **touch** this door. 译

town 市镇
I live in a small **town** in England. 译

traffic 车流，交通
The cars are crossing a road with heavy **traffic**. 译

trap 陷阱
It's a **trap**. 译

treasure 宝藏
The boy finds an island full of **treasures**. 译

true 真实的，对的
Tell me whether the following statements are **true** or false. 译

52

trunk 树干
This **trunk** is very thick. 译

try 尝试
Have a **try**, Liu Tao. 译

tuck shop 小卖部
British children often go to a **tuck shop** after school. 译

turkey 火鸡
The **turkey** says: "Gobble, gobble." 译

turn 转动
The wheels of the car began to **turn**. 译

turtle 海龟
Turtles live long. 译

Uu

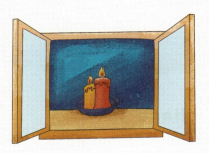

twinkle 闪烁
We saw the **twinkle** of a candle in the window. 译

ugly 丑陋的
Bob has the **ugly** habit of littering peels everywhere. 译

umbrella 雨伞
I have my **umbrella** back. 译

uniform 制服
We have to wear a school **uniform**. 译

unkind 不友好的
It was **unkind** of you not to invite her. 译

53

untidy 凌乱的，不整洁的
Don't make your room **untidy**. 译

upstairs 楼上
When you go **upstairs**, bring these towels with you. 译

use 用
I **use** my pen every day. 译

Vv

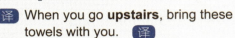
vacuum 真空
A pump was used to create a **vacuum** inside the bottle. 译

van 厢式货车
The **van** suddenly turned over. 译

very 很，非常
He likes singing and dancing **very** much. 译

vet 兽医
The little boy wishes to be a **vet** in the future. 译

village 村庄
In front of the mountain there is a small **village**. 译

visit 探望
I'm going to **visit** my grandparents. 译

voice 声音
They hear an old woman's **voice** in the house. 译

volcano 火山
This **volcano** is active. 译

Ww

wait 等
We must **wait** for our classmates.

wake 醒来
It was already 8 o'clock when he **woke** up.

walk 走，散步
They are **walking** on a bridge.

wall 墙壁
Look! The bee is on the **wall** now.

wand 魔法棒
The fairy waved her magic **wand**.

want 要
I **want** a new football, please.

warm 温暖
It's **warm** inside.

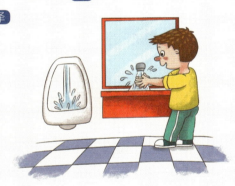

waste 浪费
We should not **waste** water.

way 路
This **way**, please.

we 我们
When **we** called him, he ran to us.

weak 虚弱的
His arms and legs were **weak**.

wear 穿
She likes to **wear** her new dress.

weather 天气
What's the **weather** like today?

web 网
The spider is spinning a **web**.

weekend 周末
On **weekends**, I go to visit my grandparents.

weigh 称重，重量
This elephant **weighs** many times more than this panda.

welcome 欢迎
Welcome to Sunshine Town.

well 很好，井
He can play basketball very **well**.

wet 湿的
They walked home in rain and were **wet** through.

what 什么
What is your name?

wheel 轮子
Jimmy fixes up broken bicycle parts, like **wheels**.

when 什么时候
When are you going home?

where 哪里
Where's Anna?

which 哪个
Which one of you is Susan?

whisker 胡子
He has dense **whiskers**.

whisper 耳语
She sat on mother's lap and **whispered** to her.

who 谁
Who is younger?

why 为什么
Why are you late?

wicked 邪恶的
She is a **wicked** witch.

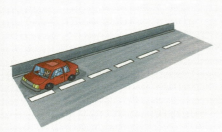
wide 宽的
The road is **wide**.

wild 野外，野生的
The animals live in the **wild**.

wild boar 野猪
This **wild boar** is stronger than a cowboy.

wipe 擦
I'm **wiping** the table.

win 赢
We **won** the game.

wire 金属线
He made the **wire** into a U shape.

57

wish 希望
How she **wished** she could have the delicious food!

witch 女巫
The old **witch** is riding on the broom.

wolf 狼
The **wolf** is standing still.

woman 妇人
Who's that **woman**?

wood 木柴
You must come with me to the forest to get some **wood**.

wool 羊毛
My mother gave me a **wool** sweater as a gift.

work 工作
I'm strong. Let's **work** together.

worker 工人
My mother is a factory **worker**.

world 世界
You'll travel around the **world**.

worm 虫
Early birds can always catch the **worms**.

worry 担心
Don't **worry**. We will do it with you.

wrap 包起来
You can **wrap** it up with paper.

wrong 错的
That picture is the **wrong** way round. 译

Xx

xylophone 木琴
The boy got down to playing **xylophone**. 译

Yy

yacht 帆船，快艇
The **yacht** is sailing. 译

year 岁，年
I'm four **years** old. 译

yell 喊叫
He is **yelling** my name. 译

yolk 蛋黄
May I have a mooncake with **yolk** inside? 译

you 你
Can I sit next to **you**? 译

Zz

zero 零
The thermometer fell to **zero** last night. 译

zoom 急速移动
Cars **zoomed** past us. 译

59

每天5分钟，单词积累不用愁

WORDS for ESL LEARNERS
情景英语4000词

④ 常用动词 1000词

沧浪文化英语创研室 ◎ 编著　　戴维·帕特里克·泰奇　王威 ◎ 审订

使用说明

为中国孩子量身定制的图画字典

纯正美音配音，给孩子最佳语感

学 习 单 词　用扫描二维码、下载MP3文件或点读的方式学习单词的正确发音。听、读例句，了解此单词的正确运用。

复 习 单 词　用"我说你做"的游戏方式帮助孩子复习所学单词。如：妈妈说中文，孩子说出英语并做出相应动作。以此熟悉单词，锻炼身体灵活性。

内容介绍

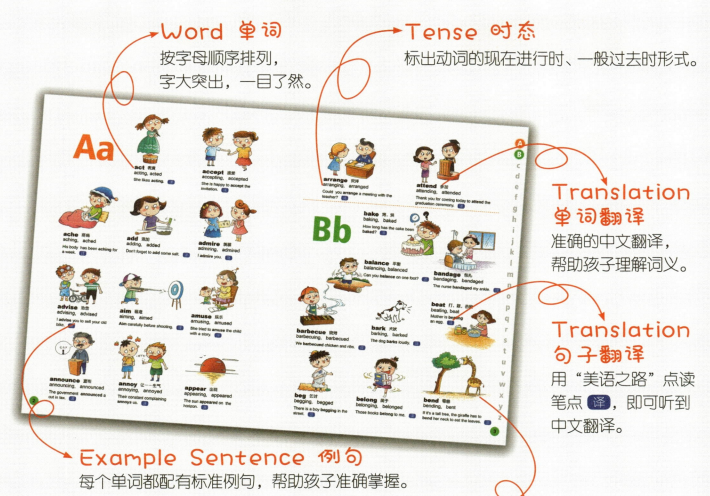

Word 单词
按字母顺序排列，字大突出，一目了然。

Tense 时态
标出动词的现在进行时、一般过去时形式。

Translation 单词翻译
准确的中文翻译，帮助孩子理解词义。

Translation 句子翻译
用"美语之路"点读笔点 译，即可听到中文翻译。

Example Sentence 例句
每个单词都配有标准例句，帮助孩子准确掌握。

Illustration 插图
生动的插图，吸引孩子注意力并帮助理解、加深记忆。

音频收听说明

朗读 贝蒂娜·朱莉

美国哥伦比亚大学表演系研究生,为"美语之路"系列图书配音,语音纯正,音质清晰。

语音评测

1. **扫码** 扫描封底的二维码,关注微信公众号。
2. **语音测评** 选择测评内容,开始录音,会有测评分数打出。

扫描二维码

1. **扫码** 扫描封底的二维码,关注"沧浪文化"公众号。
2. **听音频** 点击公众号右下角的"微课和音频",选择收听本书音频。

下载 MP3 文件

1. **进入官网** 百度搜索"沧浪文化书馨网"。
2. **下载** 点击首页右上角的"下载专区",下载本书 MP3 文件。

点读

- 本书支持:"小达人"和"美语之路"点读笔(需另购)。
- 正文中的文字和图片都可以点读。

① 打开电源开关　　② 点击封面　　③ 点读正文中的学习内容

目录 Contents

- 2　A a
- 3　B b
- 5　C c
- 12　D d

- 17　E e
- 19　F f
- 23　G g
- 27　H h

- 31　I i
- 32　J j
- 33　K k
- 34　L l

- 37　M m
- 39　N n
- 40　O o
- 41　P p

- 46　Q q
- 46　R r
- 51　S s
- 63　T t
- 67　U u

- 68　V v
- 68　W w
- 71　Y y
- 71　Z z

Aa

act 表演
acting, acted

She likes **acting**. 译

accept 接受
accepting, accepted

She is happy to **accept** the invitation. 译

ache 疼痛
aching, ached

His body has been **aching** for a week. 译

add 添加
adding, added

Don't forget to **add** some salt. 译

admire 羡慕
admiring, admired

I **admire** you. 译

advise 劝告
advising, advised

I **advise** you to sell your old bike. 译

aim 瞄准
aiming, aimed

Aim carefully before shooting. 译

amuse 娱乐
amusing, amused

She tried to **amuse** the child with a story. 译

announce 宣布
announcing, announced

The government **announced** a cut in tax. 译

annoy 让……生气
annoying, annoyed

Their constant complaining **annoys** us. 译

appear 出现
appearing, appeared

The sun **appeared** on the horizon. 译

arrange 安排
arranging, arranged

Could you **arrange** a meeting with the teacher?

attend 参加
attending, attended

Thank you for coming today to **attend** the graduation ceremony.

Bb

bake 烤, 烘
baking, baked

How long has the cake been **baked**?

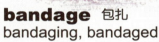
balance 平衡
balancing, balanced

Can you **balance** on one foot?

bandage 包扎
bandaging, bandaged

The nurse **bandaged** my ankle.

barbecue 烧烤
barbecuing, barbecued

We **barbecued** chicken and ribs.

bark 犬吠
barking, barked

The dog **barks** loudly.

beat 打, 敲, 击败
beating, beat

Mother is **beating** an egg.

beg 乞讨
begging, begged

There is a boy **begging** in the street.

belong 属于
belonging, belonged

These books **belong** to me.

bend 弯曲
bending, bent

If it's a tall tree, the giraffe has to **bend** its neck to eat the leaves.

bite 咬
biting, bit

The dog **bit** me. 译

bleed 流血
bleeding, bled

If your finger gets cut, it will **bleed**. 译

block 阻塞
blocking, blocked

The ambulance was **blocked** by traffic. 译

blow out 吹灭

The boy made a wish and **blew out** the candles. 译

blow up 吹气，爆炸

The little boy **blew up** a balloon. 译

blush 脸红
blushing, blushed

I **blushed** to admit it. 译

boil 沸腾
boiling, boiled

Is the kettle **boiling**? 译

borrow 借入
borrowing, borrowed

Could I **borrow** that book? 译

bounce 弹跳
bouncing, bounced

Tell the children not to **bounce** up and down on the bed. 译

box 拳击
boxing, boxed

At school I **boxed** and played basketball. 译

break 打破，折断
breaking, broke

He managed to **break** the net. 译

break down 损坏

Their car **broke down**. 译

breathe 呼吸
breathing, breathed

The patient began to **breathe** normally.

brush 刷，梳
brushing, brushed

I **brush** my teeth at ten thirty.

build 建造
building, built

I am going to **build** a new house.

bully 欺负
bullying, bullied

She **bullied** her younger brother.

bump 撞
bumping, bumped

He **bumped** up against a chair.

burn 燃烧
burning, burnt

There was a fire **burning** in the large fireplace.

burst 爆炸
bursting, burst

The balloon will **burst**.

bury 埋葬
burying, buried

She **buried** her dead pet rabbit in the backyard.

buy 买
buying, bought

Honey, let's **buy** some fruit.

button 扣上纽扣
buttoning, buttoned

Button up your overcoat.

Cc

call for 呼喊

They are **calling for** help.

call off 取消

He has **called off** the trip.

care 照顾，关心
caring, cared

We need to **care** for these plants. 译

carve 雕刻
carving, carved

He **carved** a statue. 译

celebrate 庆祝
celebrating, celebrated

what is the man **celebrating** about? 译

chat 聊天
chatting, chatted

Write to me or **chat** with me. 译

carry 携带
carrying, carried

Our spacecraft is too slow to **carry** large number of passengers to Mars. 译

catch 抓住，接住
catching, caught

I jumped up to **catch** a ball and fell over. 译

charge 冲向
charging, charged

They came **charging** into the room. 译

cheat 作弊，欺骗
cheating, cheated

They were trying to **cheat** the emperor. 译

carry on 继续进行

More money is needed to **carry on** with our work. 译

cause 引起，造成
causing, caused

All these activities can **cause** a lot of stress for children. 译

chase 追赶
chasing, chased

Maybe our cat is **chasing** a mouse now! 译

check 检查，查看
checking, checked

Check the spelling and grammatical mistakes. 译

check in 登记
Where do I have to **check in**? 译

check out 办理退房手续
They packed and **checked out** of the hotel. 译

cheer 欢呼，为……加油
cheering, cheered
The mother is **cheering** for her daughter. 译

cheer up 让……开心
The girl visited the sick kids in the hospital to **cheer** them **up**. 译

chew 咀嚼
chewing, chewed
Daniel **chewed** his apple on the sofa. 译

chip 削
chipping, chipped
Chip away the damaged area. 译

circle 旋转，画圈
circling, circled
Please **circle** the words with "-er". 译

clean 清扫
cleaning, cleaned
Let me **clean** the window. 译

clean up 打扫干净
Nina and Mary were **cleaning up** after dinner in the kitchen. 译

clear 变清澈
clearing, cleared
The early morning mist **cleared**. 译

clear off 离开
Tell the onlookers to **clear off** so that the police can do their work. 译

clear out 迅速离开
He **cleared out** without paying his rent. 译

cling 紧贴
clinging, clung

The children **clung** together under the little umbrella waiting for the storm to pass. 译

clip 夹住
clipping, clipped

He **clipped** the keys to his belt. 译

cluck 咯咯叫
clucking, clucked

The hen **clucked** at her chicks. 译

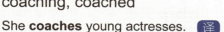

coach 训练
coaching, coached

She **coaches** young actresses. 译

coil 卷起
coiling, coiled

He **coiled** a rope. 译

collapse 倒下来
collapsing, collapsed

She came home from work and **collapsed** on to the sofa. 译

collide 撞上
colliding, collided

The car **collided** into a tree. 译

color 涂色
coloring, colored

I **colored** the rainbow in red, blue and yellow. 译

comb 梳
combing, combed

He **combed** back his hair. 译

come 来
coming, came

I hope you can **come** and share with us. 译

come across 发现

By chance I **came across** an article about this doctor. 译

come apart 裂开

This table is **coming apart**. 译

come back 回来
He waited until his father **came back** home. 译

come off 成功，脱落
It was a good try but it didn't quite **come off**. 译

come on 来吧
Come on, Susan. Let's dance. 译

come out 出来
Luckily, the sun **came out** again. 译

complain 抱怨
complaining, complained

The students **complained** that the test was too hard. 译

confuse 使迷惑
confusing, confused

The general was trying to **confuse** the enemy. 译

congratulate 祝贺
congratulating, congratulated

I'd like to **congratulate** all the students who are here today. 译

connect 连接
connecting, connected

Connect the cable to the battery. 译

consider 考虑，认为
considering, considered

Why not **consider** going to New York? 译

consist 组成
consisting, consisted

A healthy diet should **consist** of wholefood. 译

construct 建造
constructing, constructed

They **constructed** a shelter out of fallen branches. 译

contain 包含
containing, contained

This drink doesn't **contain** any sugar. 译

continue 继续
continuing, continued

I will **continue** travelling by boat. 译

contribute 做出贡献
contributing, contributed

You all **contributed** to the success of the project. 译

cool 冷却
cooling, cooled

Allow the cake to **cool** before slicing. 译

cool down 变凉

Let the glass of hot water **cool down**. 译

cool off 降温

We dived into the river to **cool off**. 译

copy 抄写，复印
copying, copied

He asked me if he could **copy** my homework. 译

cost 花费
costing, cost

Bike riding doesn't **cost** anything. 译

cough 咳嗽
coughing, coughed

The dust made her **cough** repeatedly. 译

cover 遮盖
covering, covered

The clouds had spread and nearly **covered** the entire sky. 译

cover up 盖起来

She quickly **covered** herself **up**. 译

crack 裂开
cracking, cracked

The statue **cracked**. 译

crash 撞上
crashing, crashed

She **crashed** the car into a tree, but no one was hurt. 译

10

crawl 爬行
crawling, crawled
The snake **crawled** into its hole. 译

create 创造，造成
creating, created
Her arrival **created** a terrible fuss. 译

creep 爬行，轻轻地走
creeping, crept
The crocodile was **creeping** along the riverbed. 译

croak 呱呱叫
croaking, croaked
Thousands of frogs **croaked**. 译

cross out 划掉
You had better **cross out** this word. 译

crouch 蹲下
crouching, crouched
The lion **crouched** in the tall grass, waiting to attack the gazelle. 译

crow 啼，叫
crowing, crowed
The boy **crowed** with delight. 译

crowd 拥挤
crowding, crowded
Hundreds of people **crowded** in the church. 译

crumble 弄碎
crumbling, crumbled
She **crumbled** the cookies into small bits. 译

crumple 崩溃
crumpling, crumpled
At the sight of blood, he **crumpled** to the ground. 译

crush 压碎
crushing, crushed
A windmill is used to **crush** grain into flour. 译

cuddle 依偎
cuddling, cuddled
Let's **cuddle** by the fire. 译

curl 卷曲
curling, curled

His hair **curls** naturally. 译

curtsy 屈膝行礼
curtsying, curtsied

They **curtsy** when the king is coming. 译

cut 切
cutting, cut

It's necessary to **cut** two holes in my mask for me to see. 译

cut out 剪出

I **cut out** a picture of a colorful balloon. 译

cut down 砍倒

People **cut down** so many trees that elephants are losing their habitat. 译

cycle 骑自行车
cycling, cycled

I can go **cycling**. 译

Dd

damage 损坏
damaging, damaged

Smoking seriously **damages** your health. 译

dance 跳舞
dancing, danced

Let's **dance** and sing a song. 译

dare 敢
daring, dared

I **dare** to answer questions in class. 译

darn 缝补
darning, darned

Would you **darn** these socks, please? 译

dash 泼溅
dashing, dashed

She **dashed** water in his face in an attempt to wake him up. 译

deal 解决
dealing, dealt

My friends could **deal** with their problems. 译

decide 决定
deciding, decided

They will **decide** who is the winner. 译

decorate 装饰
decorating, decorated

People **decorate** their homes. 译

defend 保卫
defending, defended

The soldiers are **defending** their country from attack. 译

delight 使高兴
delighting, delighted

The toy **delighted** the children. 译

deliver 投递，送
delivering, delivered

The baby was safely **delivered** to his mother. 译

demand 要求
demanding, demanded

She **demanded** to see the manager. 译

demonstrate 示范，说明
demonstrating, demonstrated

Your posture is not right. Let me **demonstrate** it for you. 译

describe 描述
describing, described

I can **describe** all the places near my home. 译

deserve 应该得到
deserving, deserved

The team **deserved** victory. 译

design 设计
designing, designed

Who **designed** the cover? 译

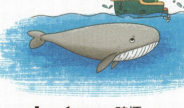

destroy 破坏
destroying, destroyed

How can a whale **destroy** a ship? 译

develop 发展,发育
developing, developed

The boy made a plan for **developing** his muscles. 译

dial 拨通
dialing, dialed

Dial 110 and ask for the police! 译

die 死
dying, died

When did Dr. Martin Luther King **die**? 译

die away 变弱

The sound **died away** and silence reigned. 译

die down 逐渐消失

The wind was **dying down** at around 3:00 a.m.. 译

dig 挖掘
digging, dug

Let's **dig** in this area for treasure. 译

direct 指挥
directing, directed

A guard **directed** them to the right. 译

disappear 消失
disappearing, disappeared

He ran after the rabbit and **disappeared**. 译

discover 发现
discovering, discovered

She **discovered** radium in their laboratory in 1898. 译

discuss 讨论
discussing, discussed

Discuss with your partner. 译

disguise 假装
disguising, disguised

She **disguised** herself as a man so she could fight in the battlefield. 译

dislike 不喜欢
disliking, disliked

They are talking about the kind of job they like or **dislike**. 译

dismiss 解雇，解散
dismissing, dismissed

She was **dismissed**. 译

display 标明，陈列
displaying, displayed

Restaurants **display** the prices on their menus. 译

disturb 打扰
disturbing, disturbed

I'm sorry to **disturb** you so late. 译

dive 跳水
diving, dived

He tried to escape by **diving** into a river. 译

divide 分
dividing, divided

Divide the sauce among 4 bowls. 译

do 做
doing, did

What did you **do** last weekend? 译

do away with 去掉

I have to **do away with** my bad habit. 译

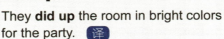

do up 装修，重新刷新

They **did up** the room in bright colors for the party. 译

dock 停靠码头
docking, docked

The ferry is expected to **dock** at 6 a.m.. 译

donate 捐出
donating, donated

We can save our pocket money and **donate** it to those in need. 译

doodle 涂画
doodling, doodled

He is **doodling** on his notebook. 译

doze 打盹
dozing, dozed

She's been **dozing** for a while. 译

drag 缓慢行进，拖拽
dragging, dragged

One of the climbers was beginning to **drag**. 译

drain 排水
draining, drained

Now the focus is on **draining** water. 译

draw 画
drawing, drew

Now let me **draw** something on it. 译

dress 打扮，穿衣服
dressing, dressed

There was an emperor who liked to **dress** in fine clothes. 译

drift 漂
drifting, drifted

We proceeded to **drift** on up the river. 译

drill 钻洞
drilling, drilled

The team is still **drilling**. 译

drink 喝
drinking, drank

What would you like to **drink**? 译

drink up 吸干

The girl **drank up** that bottle of milk. 译

drip 漏
dripping, dripped

The cracked bottle is **dripping**. 译

drive 开车
driving, drove

Tom can **drive**. 译

drop 掉，投下
dropping, dropped

Drop the noodles into the water. 译

drown 淹没
drowning, drowned

The girl almost **drowned** in the river. 译

dry 擦干
drying, dried
Dry with a soft towel. 译

dry out 变干
If the soil **dries out** the tree will die. 译

duck 让，躲避
ducking, ducked
Hans **ducked** the blows. 译

drop off 减少，下车
My interest in photography **dropped off**, and I like drawing now. 译

dump 倒掉
dumping, dumped
They can't **dump** the trash on the curb. 译

dust 拂去灰尘
dusting, dusted
The mother is **dusting** the furniture. 译

Ee

earn 赚取
earning, earned
She **earns** a good salary. 译

eat 吃
eating, ate
It's time for dinner. Let's **eat**. 译

eat up 吃光
Hobo, you've **eaten up** my breakfast. 译

edge 慢慢移动
edging, edged
Emily **edged** her chair forward. 译

elect 选举，选择
electing, elected
We are going to **elect** a new leader. 译

embarrass 使……难为情
embarrassing, embarrassed
I was really **embarrassed**. 译

embrace 拥抱
embracing, embraced
He **embraced** her warmly. 译

emerge 冒出来
emerging, emerged
Some ideas **emerged** after class. 译

employ 雇用
employing, employed
A new factory will **employ** 500 people. 译

empty 清空
emptying, emptied
You'd better **empty** the room before starting to paint the ceiling. 译

end 结束
ending, ended
In 2016, he **ended** his basketball career. 译

engrave 刻上
engraving, engraved
His name was **engraved** on the silver cup. 译

enter 进入
entering, entered
She decided to **enter** the garden. 译

entertain 娱乐
entertaining, entertained
Could you help me **entertain** the kids while I leave and prepare dinner? 译

equal 等于，等同
equaling, equaled
His salary **equals** mine. 译

erase 擦掉
erasing, erased
How to **erase** the red line on the book? 译

escape 逃走
escaping, escaped
I **escaped** from the crowd. 译

examine 检查
examining, examined

He **examined** her passport and stamped it. 译

exchange 交换
exchanging, exchanged

I'd like to **exchange** this sweater for one of a larger size. 译

excite 使……兴奋
exciting, excited

The ideas **excite** young people. 译

excuse 抱歉
excusing, excused

Excuse me. What time is it? 译

expand 扩大
expanding, expanded

They plan to **expand** the airport. 译

expect 预计,期望
expecting, expected

What can you **expect** to learn from the news? 译

explain 解释
explaining, explained

The teacher is **explaining** to the girl how to spell. 译

explore 探索,仔细看
exploring, explored

I decided to go out and **explore** the town. 译

Ff

face 面对
facing, faced

Just **face** them heroically, and you will surely win! 译

face up 勇敢面对

I can **face up** to my fears. 译

fade 褪色,变弱
fading, faded

The light **faded** as the sun went down. 译

faint 晕倒
fainting, fainted

I think I am going to **faint**. 译

fake 伪造,假装
faking, faked

The test results were **faked**. 译

fall 落下
falling, fell

September had come and the leaves were starting to **fall**. 译

fall off 摔倒
She **fell** off on the seashore. 译

fan 扇风
fanning, fanned

He **fanned** himself with a piece of newspaper. 译

fast 禁食
fasting, fasted

Patients must **fast** for six hours before having an operation. 译

farm 耕种
farming, farmed

They **farm** trees for fuel. 译

fasten 固定住
fastening, fastened

He **fastened** the dog's leash to a post and went into the store. 译

fear 害怕
fearing, feared

There's no need to **fear**. 译

feed 喂
feeding, fed

I can **feed** her carrots and I like her long ears. 译

feel like 想要

Do you **feel like** a walk? 译

fence 围起来
fencing, fenced

He **fenced** in the sheep. 译

fetch 取回
fetching, fetched

If you throw the ball the dog will **fetch** it. 译

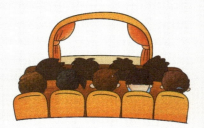
fill up 装满

The theatre began to **fill up** just before the performance. 译

find 找到
finding, found

He can help the boys **find** the Italian restaurant. 译

find out 查明，知道

I hope to **find out** what's going on around the world. 译

finish with 断绝，完成

I've **finished with** gambling. 译

fire 燃烧，开枪
firing, fired

After drying, china clay are **fired** at a very high heat. 译

fish 钓鱼
fishing, fished

Mr. Brown plans to go **fishing** after work. 译

fit 适合
fitting, fitted

This key **fits** the lock. 译

fit in 容得下

How many people can **fit in** a phone booth? 译

fix 修理，准备
fixing, fixed

Could you **fix** your robot yourself? 译

fizz 发出嘶嘶声
fizzing, fizzed

The soda **fizzed**. 译

flag 变弱
flagging, flagged

Her interest in music has begun to **flag**. 译

flap 飘
flapping, flapped

The sheets were **flapping**. 译

flash 闪亮
flashing, flashed

A message **flashed** on the screen. 译

flatten 弄平
flattening, flattened

Flatten the dough with a press of hand. 译

flee 逃跑
fleeing, fled

The thief **fled**. 译

flick 轻拂
flicking, flicked

She **flicked** her hair back over her shoulder. 译

fling 扔
flinging, flung

They **flung** their hats into the air. 译

flip 翻转
flipping, flipped

His car **flipped** over on the interstate. 译

flit 快速移动
flitting, flitted

She was always **flitting** in the kitchen. 译

float 漂浮
floating, floated

The bamboo raft **floated** downstream. 译

flood 溢出，淹没
flooding, flooded

The river will soon **flood** the bank. 译

flow 流
flowing, flowed

She opened the faucet and the water began to **flow**. 译

fluff 使松散
fluffing, fluffed

The wind **fluffed** her hair. 译

flush 冲洗
flushing, flushed

The boy can **flush** the toilet by himself. 译

foam 起泡
foaming, foamed

The boiling soup was **foaming**. 译

fold 折叠
folding, folded

Could you **fold** the clothes? 译

follow 跟随
following, followed

Follow me, please! 译

form 出现，构成
forming, formed

Storm clouds are **forming** on the horizon. 译

freeze 冻住
freezing, froze

The cold weather **froze** the water pipes. 译

frighten 害怕
frightening, frightened

He was too **frightened** to know what to do. 译

frown 皱眉
frowning, frowned

She was **frowning** when she entered the room. 译

fry 油炸，油煎
frying, fried

We could smell the onions **frying**. 译

Gg

gallop 飞奔
galloping, galloped

The horse **galloped** toward us. 译

gamble 赌博
gambling, gambled

Many people visit Las Vegas to **gamble** their hard-earned money. 译

garden 在园中种植
gardening, gardened

Gardening is my hobby. 译

gasp 喘气
gasping, gasped

He **gasped** for air above the surface of the water. 译

gather 聚集
gathering, gathered

Many tourists like to **gather** there to watch the sunrise. 译

gaze 注视
gazing, gazed
She **gazed** intently into his eyes. 译

get up 起床
When do you **get up**? I often **get up** at 7 o'clock. 译

get across 通过
The bridge was destroyed, so we couldn't **get across**. 译

get along
与……和谐相处，前进
Can you **get along** with your roommate? 译

get around 到处走走
It's easy for people to **get around** now. 译

get at 得到
A goat was standing up against a tree on its forelegs trying to **get at** the leaves. 译

get back 回来
When did you **get back** from your vacation? 译

get down 下来
The boy was **getting down** from the plane. 译

get dressed 穿衣
It's time to get out of bed and **get dressed**. 译

get in 进入
She **got in** Durham University to study law. 译

get into 陷入
They do not want to **get into** trouble. 译

get off 下车
Don't **get off** until the car stops. 译

get on 继续进行
Jane **got on** with her work.

get over 克服
I'm sure she will **get over** it.

giggle 咯咯笑
giggling, giggled
She **giggled** like a little kid.

give away 赠送，失去
I **gave away** my bike to a children's home.

give back 归还
The teacher **gave back** his test paper.

give out 分发，公布
The teacher **gave out** the examination papers.

give up 放弃，自首
Yu Gong kept trying and didn't **give up**.

glare 发出刺眼的光，瞪
glaring, glared
The sun **glared** on the sea.

glide 滑翔，滑行
gliding, glided
We watched the skiers **gliding** down the slope.

glow 发光，发热
glowing, glowed
The coals **glowed** in the fireplace.

glue 盯着，粘贴
gluing, glued
All eyes are **glued** to the TV screen.

go 去
going, went
Can I **go** outside now?

go away 走开

She told him to **go away** and stop bothering her. 译

go back 回去

Go back inside, or you'll catch cold. 译

go on 继续，向前走

If you **go on** like that, you will be in danger. 译

go out 出去

She enjoys **going out** on weekends. 译

go without 没有……也行

I can't **go without** sleep. 译

grab 抓，抢夺
grabbing, grabbed

Jim **grabbed** a cake from the plate. 译

greet 迎接，问候
greeting, greeted

Most people around the world now **greet** each other by shaking hands. 译

grill 烤
grilling, grilled

Grill the sausages for ten minutes. 译

grin 咧嘴笑
grinning, grinned

She **grinned** at the kids playing in the pool. 译

grind 磨
grinding, ground

The corn is **ground** into flour. 译

grip 紧握，抓住
gripping, gripped

The little boy **gripped** his mother's hand tightly. 译

grunt 发出呼噜声，咕哝
grunting, grunted

The pig is **grunting**. 译

guard 看守
guarding, guarded
Two policemen were assigned to **guard** the prisoner. 译

guess 猜
guessing, guessed
Could your classmates **guess** what it is? 译

guide 引导
guiding, guided
Bea **guided** the guests in the museum. 译

gum 粘贴
gumming, gummed
Don't use that paper with the copier, or you'll **gum** it up. 译

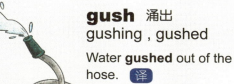
gush 涌出
gushing, gushed
Water **gushed** out of the hose. 译

Hh

hack 砍
hacking, hacked
I **hacked** the dead branches off. 译

hail 呼叫
hailing, hailed
We **hailed** the passing ship. 译

halt 停止，立定
halting, halted
The colonel ordered the soldiers to **halt**. 译

halve 分成两半
halving, halved
He **halved** the sandwich. 译

hammer 敲打
hammering, hammered
The carpenters were **hammering** all afternoon. 译

handle 操作
handling, handled
He knows how to **handle** a motorcycle. 译

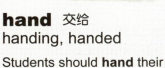
hand 交给
handing, handed
Students should **hand** their composition in on Thursday. 译

hand out 分发
She **handed** flyers **out** at the grocery store. 译

27

harm 伤害
harming, harmed

Too much sunshine can **harm** your skin. 译

harvest 收割
harvesting, harvested

It is time to **harvest** the wheat. 译

hatch 孵出，出壳
hatching, hatched

Two chicks **hatched** this morning. 译

hate 憎恨，厌恶
hating, hated

He **hates** swimming. 译

haul 拖
hauling, hauled

They **hauled** the boat up onto the beach. 译

have 拥有
having, had

It is their dream to **have** a bridge. 译

have to 必须

Does he **have to** wear a uniform at school? 译

head 用头顶
heading, headed

He **headed** the ball to make a shot. 译

heal 治愈
healing, healed

It took a long time for the wounds to **heal**. 译

heap 堆
heaping, heaped

Rocks were **heaped** up on the side of the road. 译

hear 听见
hearing, heard

Sorry, I didn't **hear** you. 译

heat 加热
heating, heated

The vegetables got **heated** in the microwave. 译

hiccup 打嗝
hiccupping, hiccupped

When you **hiccup**, drink a glass of cold water. 译

hide 躲藏
hiding, hid

I guess the children are **hiding** behind the wall. 译

hike 徒步行走
hiking, hiked

He **hiked** ten miles through the forest. 译

hire 租用
hiring, hired

It is also popular to **hire** a bicycle and ride around the countryside. 译

hiss 发出嘘声
hissing, hissed

The audience **hissed** him off the stage. 译

hit 击打
hitting, hit

She **hit** the ball too hard and it went out of the court. 译

hoist 吊起，升起
hoisting, hoisted

The cargo was **hoisted** up onto the ship. 译

hold 握住
holding, held

Hold the rail so you won't fall. 译

hold on 等，忍受，坚持

Hold on a minute, for it's not your turn. 译

hold out 抵挡，伸出

How long can we **hold out** against these attacks? 译

hold up 阻挡，举起

The traffic was **held up** for miles by the accident. 译

honk 鹅叫
honking, honked

We could hear the geese **honking** overhead. 译

hook 勾住
hooking, hooked

My sweater was **hooked** unto a branch. 译

hoot 鸣响
hooting, hooted

The train **hooted** a warning. 译

hope 希望
hoping, hoped

I **hope** you can come and share some cakes with us. 译

hop 跳跃
hopping, hopped

He **hopped** over the hot sand. 译

hose 用软管浇水
hosing, hosed

We wash our car and **hose** our garden. 译

howl 嚎叫，大声哭
howling, howled

The dogs were **howling** at the moon. 译

huff 喘气
huffing, huffed

He **huffed** and puffed as he made his way up the mountain. 译

hug 拥抱
hugging, hugged

He **hugged** them warmly. 译

hum 发出嗡嗡声
humming, hummed

The garden was **humming** with bees. 译

hunt 猎食，找
hunting, hunted

Lions sometimes **hunt** alone. 译

hurl 用力抛
hurling, hurled

He **hurled** a chair at me. 译

hurry 抓紧，急忙
hurrying, hurried

The kids **hurried** to open their presents. 译

hurry up 赶快

Hurry up! We're going to be late!

hurt 受伤
hurting, hurt

I fell off my bike and **hurt** my foot.

Ii

imagine 想象
imagining, imagined

I **imagine** myself flying like a bird.

imitate 模仿
imitating, imitated

He's very good at **imitating** his father's voice.

increase 增加
increasing, increased

The population continues to **increase**.

inform 通知
informing, informed

Please **inform** us of any changes of address.

injure 受伤
injuring, injured

She fell and **injured** herself.

inspect 检查
inspecting, inspected

After the storm, we went outside to **inspect** the damage.

install 安装
installing, installed

We thought about **installing** a new phone system.

instruct 指导, 教
instructing, instructed

He **instructed** me in nursing techniques.

interrupt 打断
interrupting, interrupted

It's not polite to **interrupt** when someone is talking. 译

interview 采访
interviewing, interviewed

Interview your classmates and then give a report. 译

introduce 介绍
introducing, introduced

In your letter, you should **introduce** yourself first. 译

invent 发明
inventing, invented

I want to **invent** a pen that can write fast. 译

iron 熨
ironing, ironed

I **ironed** the shirt. 译

itch 发痒
itching, itched

This sweater makes me **itch**. 译

Jj

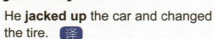
jack up 顶起

He **jacked up** the car and changed the tire. 译

jam 塞进
jamming, jammed

People continued to **jam** into the crowded hall. 译

jerk 痉挛，颤动
jerking, jerked

The patient's legs were **jerking**. 译

jingle 叮当响
jingling, jingled

Her bracelets **jingled** like bells. 译

jog 慢跑
jogging, jogged

Local people like **jogging** in the park. 译

jot 匆匆记下，速记
jotting, jotted

He paused to **jot** a few notes on a slip of paper. 译

judge 判断
judging, judged

You should not **judge** people by their appearance. 译

juggle 玩杂耍，欺骗
juggling, juggled

My uncle taught me to **juggle**. 译

jumble 弄乱
jumbling, jumbled

He **jumbled** the wires up when he moved the TV. 译

jump 跳跃
jumping, jumped

My dad started to **jump** up and down in the tent. 译

jump at 欣然接受

He **jumped at** the offer of a better job. 译

jump up 向上跳

The basketball player **jumps up** and grab the ball. 译

Kk

keep 保持
keeping, kept

I asked them to **keep** quiet. 译

keep away 离开，不接近

He **keeps away** from liquor and tobacco. 译

keep off 远离

I **keep off** drugs. 译

keep up 跟上

He lengthened his stride to **keep up** with his father. 译

kick 踢
kicking, kicked

He **kicked** the ball into the goal. 译

kill 杀死
killing, killed

Poachers **kill** elephants for their ivories. 译

kiss 亲吻
kissing, kissed

Mother usually **kisses** Tom's cheek. 译

kneel 跪下
kneeling, kneeled

She was **kneeling** on the floor beside her child. 译

knit 编织
knitting, knitted

He likes to **knit**. 译

knot 打结
knotting, knotted

Knot the threads together. 译

Ll

ladle 舀
ladling, ladled

The soup was **ladled** into the bowls. 译

land 降落
landing, landed

We watched the seaplanes **landing** on the water. 译

lay 放置
laying, laid

He **laid** the newspaper down on the desk. 译

lead up to 通向

The path **leads up to** the hill. 译

leak 漏
leaking, leaked

The roof is **leaking**. 译

lean 斜靠
leaning, leaned

The boy **leaned** his head on his mother's shoulder. 译

leap 跳跃，飞跃
leaping, leaped

One small step for a man, one giant **leap** for mankind. 译

leave 离开
leaving, left

It is time to **leave** our school. 译

lend 借出
lending, lent

Could you **lend** me some money? 译

let 让
letting, let

Father **let** me play with the puppy. 译

let down 放下

Please **let down** the blinds. 译

let go 放开，松手

Let go of the door handle, please. 译

let in 让……进来

The interstices between the bricks **let in** cold air. 译

let out 发出

She **let out** a scream. 译

lick 舔
licking, licked

The dog jumped on to him and **licked** him. 译

lie 说谎
lying, lied

Don't **lie** to me! 译

lie down 躺下

If you have stomachache, you should **lie down** and rest. 译

lift 举起
lifting, lifted

I **lifted** my left hand into the air. 译

light 照亮，点燃
lighting, lighted

They used candles to **light** the room. 译

like 喜欢
liking, liked

Do you **like** this skirt? It's very pretty. 译

limp 一拐一拐地走
limping, limped

The injured player **limped** off the court. 译

line 画线
lining, lined

He **lined** on a white paper with a pen. 译

line up 排队

The students **lined up** after the teacher. 译

link 连接
linking, linked

The railway **links** between Beijing and Shanghai. 译

list 列出
listing, listed

I **listed** my likes and dislikes. 译

litter 乱丢
littering, littered

No **littering**. 译

live 生存
living, lived

Camels **live** in very dry places. 译

live on 靠……生活

Now pandas have less and less bamboos to **live on**. 译

load 装载
loading, loaded

We **loaded** the car and drove off. 译

lock 锁上
locking, locked

She **locked** the door. 译

lock up 锁住

He **locked up** the shop and went home. 译

look 看
looking, looked

Look at the pictures. 译

look for 寻找
He went out to **look for** his horse.

look up 查找
I **look up** new words in a dictionary.

love 喜欢，爱慕
loving, loved
They both **love** riding bikes.

look out 小心
Look out!

look after 照看
Dogs can **look after** our homes.

loop 使……成环
looping, looped
She **looped** a string around her finger.

listen 听
listening, listened
Do you often **listen** to music on weekends?

Mm

make for 前往
After he left the office he **made** straight **for** home.

make off 离开
The ship **made off** port.

make out 理解
I could **make out** what she said.

march 行进
marching, marched
They **marched** 20 miles to reach the capital.

mark 做标记
marking, marked
She **marked** an "X" on each box.

marry 结婚
marrying, married

She **married** a French scientist called Pierre Curie in 1895. 译

mash 捣碎
mashing, mashed

She **mashed** the potatoes. 译

match 相配
matching, matched

Match the words in the box with the signs. 译

measure 测量
measuring, measured

He is **measuring** the man. He is a good tailor. 译

melt 融化
melting, melted

The butter **melted** in the frying pan. 译

mend 修理
mending, mended

Dad is trying to **mend** the roof. 译

mess up 弄乱

Don't **mess up** my room. 译

mew 咪咪叫
mewing, mewed

We heard the cats **mewing** in the field. 译

milk 挤奶
milking, milked

She is **milking** a cow. 译

mime 模仿
miming, mimed

He is **miming** the woman who is cleaning the floor. 译

mince 切碎
mincing, minced

She **minced** the onions. 译

miss out 漏掉

Don't **miss out** anything! 译

mistake 误解，弄错
mistaking, mistook

They **mistook** my meaning. 译

model 当模特儿
modelling, modelled

She began **modelling** in Paris at 15. 译

moo 哞哞叫
mooing, mooed

We heard the cows **mooing** in the field. 译

mop 擦掉
mopping, mopped

Please **mop** up the mess. 译

mount 骑上
mounting, mounted

He **mounted** the horse and rode away. 译

move in 搬进

I **moved in** a new apartment. 译

move out 搬出

We **moved out** of our old house. 译

mow 割
mowing, mowed

They are **mowing** the lawn. 译

Nn

nail 钉住
nailing, nailed

Nail the picture onto the wall. 译

name 命名
naming, named

The magazine *Reading* **named** him among the top 100 teachers. 译

nap 打盹
napping, napped
He's **napping** in the couch. 译

neigh 马嘶，嘶叫
neighing, neighed
We heard a distant **neigh**. 译

net 用网捕
netting, netted
We **netted** nine fish during the trip. 译

nibble 啃，小口咬
nibbling, nibbled
We **nibbled** on cheese and crackers. 译

nip 咬
nipping, nipped
He winced as the dog **nipped** his ankle. 译

nod 点头
nodding, nodded
Ahmed Aziz **nodded** at the girls. 译

notice 注意到
noticing, noticed
Luckily, I'd **noticed** where you left the car. 译

nudge 轻轻推
nudging, nudged
I **nudged** the plate closer to him. 译

nurse 照料
nursing, nursed
The mother **nursed** her sick son. 译

Oo

obey 遵守
obeying, obeyed
We should **obey** traffic rules. 译

occupy 占用
occupying, occupied
They **occupy** the room next to ours. 译

offer 提供
offering, offered

Can you **offer** me some suggestions? 译

oil 加油，涂油
oiling, oiled

The boy **oiled** the apparatus. 译

open 打开
opening, opened

I can **open** the door. 译

operate 动手术，运转
operating, operated

The machine can **operate** at high speeds. 译

order 点菜
ordering, ordered

I can **order** food in a restaurant in English. 译

overtake 赶上，超车
overtaking, overtook

It's dangerous to **overtake** on a bend. 译

overturn 打翻
overturning, overturned

The dog **overturned** the bowl. 译

owe 欠
owing, owed

Thanks for sticking up for me. I **owe** you one. 译

own 拥有
owning, owned

Bob **owns** a robot. 译

Pp

pack up 打包，整理

Oh, it's time to **pack up** my clothes. 译

paddle 用桨划
paddling, paddled

We **paddled** the canoe along the coast. 译

41

pant 喘气
panting, panted
She finished the race **panting** heavily. 译

parachute 跳伞
parachuting, parachuted
She regularly goes **parachuting**. 译

park 停车
parking, parked
You can **park** your car here. 译

pass 传递
passing, passed
We **pass** on information with letters. 译

paste 粘贴
pasting, pasted
They **paste** couplets with lucky words on the door. 译

pat 轻拍
patting, patted
The child gently **patted** the dog on the head. 译

patch 修补
patching, patched
The fence needs to be **patched**. 译

patrol 巡逻
patrolling, patrolled
Police **patrol** the streets. 译

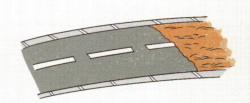
pave 铺设
paving, paved
The driveway is **paved** with concrete. 译

paw 用爪子抓，扒
pawing, pawed
The bull was **pawing** the dirt. 译

pay back 偿还，支付
He **paid** the money **back** promptly. 译

peck 啄
pecking, pecked
A crow **pecked** at the lawn, hunting for bugs. 译

pedal 骑自行车，踩……踏板
pedaling, pedaled

He **pedals** as fast as me. 译

peel 剥皮
peeling, peeled

First, **peel** the banana. 译

peep 慢慢露出
peeping, peeped

Early spring flowers were **peeping** through the snow. 译

peg 夹住
pegging, pegged

All their wet clothes were **pegged** onto the line. 译

perform 表演
performing, performed

Can you **perform** ballet? 译

pick 采摘
picking, picked

She **picked** some strawberries. 译

pick out 挑选出

I've **picked out** the perfect spot for our picnic. 译

pick up 捡起

Ridley **picked up** a pencil. 译

pin 钉住
pinning, pinned

He **pinned** a notice to the door. 译

pinch 捏
pinching, pinched

He **pinched** the baby's cheeks playfully. 译

place 放置
placing, placed

Place the mirror against the wall. 译

play 玩，演奏
playing, played

It's 2 o'clock. Let's **play** football. 译

plough 犁，耕
ploughing, ploughed

They **ploughed** nearly 100 acres of the land.

pluck 拔，拽
plucking, plucked

My sister **plucked** a white hair from my head.

point out 指出

Could you **point out** the restrooms, please.

poke 拨开，捅
poking, poked

She **poked** the sand with her toes.

polish 打磨，抛光
polishing, polished

They are **polished** and then painted.

pose 摆姿势
posing, posed

The six girls **posed** for photographs.

post 邮寄
posting, posted

I don't know when I'll **post** the letter for you.

pounce 扑过去
pouncing, pounced

The cat crouched low and waited for the moment to **pounce**.

pound 猛击
pounding, pounded

Heavy waves **pounded** the shore.

pour 倒，流出
pouring, poured

He carefully **poured** the water into her glass.

powder 擦粉
powdering, powdered

She **powdered** her face.

practice 练习
practicing, practiced

I want to **practice** the song.

praise 表扬，称赞
praising, praised
The cave is **praised** as the "Art Palace of Nature". 译

prepare 准备，筹备
preparing, prepared
She has **prepared** some books for children. 译

present 赠送，颁发
presenting, presented
A medal was **presented** to the winner at the games. 译

press 按压
pressing, pressed
She **pressed** the pieces of clay together. 译

pretend 假装
pretending, pretended
He **pretended** that he did not know the answer. 译

prick 刺
pricking, pricked
The nurse **pricked** my finger and squeezed out a drop of blood. 译

print 印刷，打印
printing, printed
He invented the technology for **printing** Chinese characters. 译

promise 承诺，答应
promising, promised
Will you **promise** to write to me? 译

protect 保护
protecting, protected
We can **protect** the environment by recycling waste. 译

pull away 离开，拉
The father **pulled** his child **away**. 译

pump 打气
pumping, pumped
I tried to **pump** up my back tire. 译

punish 惩罚
punishing, punished
Bob was **punished** for being naughty. 译

purr （猫）发出呼噜声
purring, purred

The cat was **purring**. 译

put away 把……收拾好

Put your books **away** in the bookcase 译

puzzle 使……困惑
puzzling, puzzled

The question **puzzled** me. 译

Qq

quack 鸭子嘎嘎叫
quacking, quacked

We could hear the ducks **quacking**. 译

quarrel 吵架
quarrelling, quarrelled

My brother **quarrelled** with my father. 译

quarter 分成四份
quartering, quartered

Chop the mushrooms and **quarter** the tomatoes. 译

question 询问
questioning, questioned

The police had been **questioning** him for three hours. 译

queue up 排队

Please **queue up** to register. 译

Rr

race 赛跑
racing, raced

Eight horses will **race** for the cup. 译

rain 下雨
raining, rained

They will go tomorrow unless it **rains**. 译

raise 筹集，抚养
raising, raised

The best way to **raise** money is to sell newspapers.

rake 用耙子耙
raking, raked

The leaves had been **raked** into a pile.

ram 猛击
ramming, rammed

She **rammed** her fist against the wall in anger.

read 阅读
reading, read

Tim is **reading** a book in the library.

record 记录，录音
recording, recorded

Please **record** the scores for me.

reflect 映现，反映
reflecting, reflected

His face was **reflected** in the mirror.

refuse 拒绝
refusing, refused

He always **refuses** to let me watch my favorite TV show.

regret 后悔
regretting, regretted

I **regretted** talking back, not listening to mom.

relate 讲述
relating, related

Father **related** a story of his friend to me.

release 救出，释放
releasing, released

Firefighters took two hours to **release** the driver from the wreckage.

remain 剩下，留下
remaining, remained

Little **remained** after the fire.

remind 提醒
reminding, reminded

My robot will **remind** you to take medicine at the right time.

remove 脱去，迁移
removing, removed

He **removed** his jacket. 译

renew 更新
renewing, renewed

My father can **renew** your driver's license online. 译

repeat 重复
repeating, repeated

This robot can **repeat** my words. 译

replace 替代，取代
replacing, replaced

Teachers will never be **replaced** by computers in the classroom. 译

report 报道
reporting, reported

It is **reported** that the new book will come out. 译

request 要求
requesting, requested

My mother **requested** me to do the dishes. 译

rescue 解救
rescuing, rescued

He **rescued** a child from drowning. 译

reserve 保留
reserving, reserved

We'll **reserve** the ticket for you till tomorrow noon. 译

reserve 预订
reserving, reserved

We **reserved** a hotel room. 译

respect 尊敬
respecting, respected

I **respect** him very much. 译

result 由……造成
resulting, resulted

The fire **resulted** from an explosion. 译

reveal 揭露，透露
revealing, revealed

It was **revealed** that they stole over 1 million dollars. 译

48

ride 骑
riding, rode
We can **ride** bicycles.

ring 响
ringing, rang
The bell **rings** and the students come into class.

ring off 挂断电话
He said he didn't have time to talk and quickly **rang off**.

ring up 打电话
Ring up the airport and find out when the plane leaves.

rip 撕
ripping, ripped
He **ripped** open the package.

rise 升起
rising, rose
Black dense smoke **rose** up.

roam 漫步，走
roaming, roamed
Goats **roam** free on the mountain.

roar 吼，喊
roaring, roared
"Watch out," he **roared**.

roast 烤
roasting, roasted
The hunters **roasted** the pig.

rob 抢劫
robbing, robbed
They **robbed** the bank.

rock 摇
rocking, rocked
She gently **rocked** the baby to sleep.

roll 滚
rolling, rolled
The ball **rolled** down the hill.

roll up 卷起

The jacket was so big for him that he **rolled up** the cuffs.

roller-skate 溜旱冰
roller-skating, roller-skated

I enjoy **roller-skating** and playing volleyball.

row 划
rowing, rowed

We can **row** a boat on the lake.

rub 擦
rubbing, rubbed

Rub the surface smooth.

rub out 擦掉

Rub out chalk marks with an eraser.

ruffle 弄乱，弄皱
ruffling, ruffled

Her hair was **ruffled** by the wind.

ruin 毁掉
ruining, ruined

Years of computer use **ruined** his eyesight.

rule 统治
ruling, ruled

The queen **ruled** for 25 years.

run 跑
running, ran

He is **running**.

run away 逃跑

Gulliver wanted to **run away**.

run into 跑进

Someone is **running into** the building.

run after 追赶，追捕

The police are **running after** the thief.

run over 碾过

The dog was **run over** by a bus and killed.

run out of 用完

We've **run out of** sugar, so I must buy some more. 译

rush 冲向
rushing, rushed

I quickly put on my uniform and **rushed** to school. 译

rust 生锈
rusting, rusted

The paint prevents **rusting**. 译

Ss

sag 下垂
sagging, sagged

The roof is **sagging** in the middle. 译

sail 航行
sailing, sailed

Simon loves **sailing** on the sea. 译

salute 致敬
saluting, saluted

We **salute** our country's soldiers. 译

save 节省
saving, saved

Taking shorter showers will **save** water. 译

save up 储蓄，攒钱

He **saved up** a lot of money. 译

scare 惊吓
scaring, scared

If you get **scared** easily, do not watch it! 译

scold 责骂
scolding, scolded

Mother **scolded** the girl for not cleaning up her room. 译

scoop 用勺子挖
scooping, scooped

She has a job **scooping** ice cream. 译

51

scoop out 挖出

The mother turtle **scoops out** a hollow in the sand.

scoop up 捞出来

I **scoop up** rocks from the river.

score 得分
scoring, scored

We cheered every time our team **scored**.

scrape 擦伤
scraping, scraped

I **scraped** my knee when I fell.

scratch 抓，挠
scratching, scratched

Will you **scratch** my back for me?

scratch out 划掉

His name was **scratched out**.

scream 尖叫
screaming, screamed

I **screamed** for help.

screw 拧紧
screwing, screwed

Screw the cap on tight.

scrub 用力擦洗
scrubbing, scrubbed

She **scrubbed** the potatoes.

seal 封住，密封
sealing, sealed

Would you **seal** this envelope?

search 搜寻
searching, searched

We **searched** for him for hours.

see 看见
seeing, saw

I can **see** with my eyes.

select 选出
selecting, selected

Please **select** one item from the list. 译

sell out 卖完

They raised money by **selling out** Christmas cards. 译

send 发送
sending, sent

She **sent** me an email last week. 译

send back 送回，退还

The girl **sent** the toy **back** to the clerk. 译

send off 罚……离场

Ken scored a goal, but later he was **sent off**. 译

separate 分开
separating, separated

The bottles are **separated** in different groups and recycled. 译

serve 供应，服务
serving, served

This restaurant **serves** the best food in town. 译

set about 开始做

They **set about** creating a new website. 译

set off 出发

Li Fang **set off** for home. 译

sew 缝纫
sewing, sewed

He was busy **sewing**. 译

shade 遮住
shading, shaded

Several large trees **shade** the house. 译

shake 摇动
shaking, shook

Shaking one's head means "disagreement" in most countries. 译

shake off 摆脱

He grabbed my arm. I **shook** him **off**.

shampoo 洗发
shampooing, shampooed

Shampoo your hair and dry it.

shape 塑造
shaping, shaped

The clay is well **shaped**.

share 分享
sharing, shared

She **shared** the cake with me.

sharpen 削尖
sharpening, sharpened

I am **sharpening** a pencil.

shave 剃
shaving, shaved

He **shaved** his head.

shear 剪
shearing, sheared

The farmers **sheared** the sheep.

shell 炮轰，剥皮
shelling, shelled

The town was **shelled** during the battle.

shelter 庇护
sheltering, sheltered

A cave **sheltered** the climbers during the storm.

shift 移动
shifting, shifted

He stopped, **shifting** his cane to his left hand.

shine 擦亮，发出光
shining, shone

Was the sun **shining**?

shiver 颤抖
shivering, shivered

He **shivered** in the cold.

shock 震惊
shocking, shocked
The children were all **shocked** to learn of the death of their headmaster. 译

shop 选购
shopping, shopped
Let's go **shopping** together! 译

shout 喊叫
shouting, shouted
The king was very angry and **shouted**, "Go away!" 译

shovel 铲
shoveling, shoveled
He is outside **shoveling** snow. 译

show off 炫耀
She is **showing off** her gift. 译

show up 出现
Mary waited an hour before Tim **showed up**. 译

shower 淋浴
showering, showered
You are dirty! Go and **shower**. 译

shrink 缩小
shrinking, shrank
The sweater **shrank** when it was washed. 译

shut 闭上，关上
shutting, shut
He **shut** his eyes and fell asleep. 译

shut up 住口
When they'd finally **shut up**, I started to speak again. 译

sign 签名
signing, signed
Sign your name on the bottom line. 译

sink 下沉
sinking, sank
The ship is **sinking**. 译

sit back 休息，向后靠着坐
He **sat back** in his chair and started to read. 译

sit down 坐下
They **sat down** under a big tree. 译

sit up 端坐
He **sat up** in bed. 译

skate 滑冰
skating, skated
I like skating but I hate to **skate** today. 译

ski 滑雪
skiing, skied
He loves to **ski**. 译

skip 跳
skipping, skipped
I **skipped** six times! 译

slap 拍打
slapping, slapped
He **slapped** me on the back and said "Good job!" 译

slice 切开，切片
slicing, sliced
She **sliced** the lemon in half. 译

slide 滑动
sliding, slid
He **slid** open the door of the glass cabinet. 译

slip 滑倒
slipping, slipped
She **slipped** on the ice. 译

slip off 脱下
Slip off your shirt and I'll take your blood pressure. 译

slope 倾斜
sloping, sloped
The bank **sloped** down sharply to the river. 译

smash 打碎
smashing, smashed

The ball **smashed** the window pane. 译

smell 闻到
smelling, smelt

We could **smell** the apple pie. 译

smile 微笑
smiling, smiled

She looked very kind and **smiled** a lot. 译

smoke 吸烟
smoking, smoked

Teenagers should not be allowed to **smoke**. 译

smooth 使……平整
smoothing, smoothed

She **smoothed** back her hair. 译

snatch 抢走
snatching, snatched

She **snatched** the toy from his hands. 译

sneeze 打喷嚏
sneezing, sneezed

Ken puts his hand over his mouth when he **sneezes**. 译

sniff 吸气，抽鼻子
sniffing, sniffed

She **sniffed** and wiped her nose with a tissue. 译

snore 打呼噜
snoring, snored

I cannot bear the noise of **snoring**. 译

snow 下雪
snowing, snowed

In Alaska, USA, it **snows** a lot. 译

soak 泡
soaking, soaked

I'm going to **soak** in the bath. 译

sob 哭泣
sobbing, sobbed

He began to **sob**. 译

sow 播种
sowing, sowed

We'll **sow** in the early spring. 译

spank 打
spanking, spanked

Parents shouldn't **spank** their children. 译

speak 说话
speaking, spoke

Can you **speak** English? 译

speed 快速前行
speeding, sped

A car was **speeding** up in the street. 译

spell 拼写
spelling, spelt

How do you **spell** this word? 译

spend 花费，度过
spending, spent

I like to **spend** time with my grandparents on Sunday. 译

spill 洒落
spilling, spilt

I accidentally **spilt** coffee all over my new suit. 译

spin 旋转
spinning, span

The spacecraft began **spinning** out of control. 译

spit 吐
spitting, spat

She took a mouthful of food and then suddenly **spat** it out. 译

splash 泼，溅湿
splashing, splashed

Don't **splash** water at your brother. 译

split 分裂
spliting, split

In a severe gale the ship **split** in two. 译

split up 劈开，分开

I **split up** the wood. 译

spoil 溺爱
spoiling, spoiled

She **spoils** those kids of hers.

spoon 用勺舀
spooning, spooned

She **spooned** the sauce over the chicken pieces.

spot 发现
spotting, spotted

Neighbours **spotted** smoke coming out of the house.

spray 喷
spraying, sprayed

She **sprayed** some perfume into the air.

spread 铺开
spreading, spread

The little girl is **spreading** a cloth on a table.

spring 出现，跳出
springing, sprang

The deer **sprang** up the path.

sprinkle 喷洒，浇
sprinkling, sprinkled

He **sprinkled** water on the plants.

squash 压扁
squashing, squashed

The tomatoes got **squashed**.

squat 蹲下
squatting, squatted

We **squatted** beside the pool and watched the diver sink slowly down.

squeeze 挤
squeezing, squeezed

Squeeze out some toothpaste on your toothbursh.

stack 叠放
stacking, stacked

She **stacked** the plates in the cupboard.

stand 站立
standing, stood

The elephant is **standing** over there!

stand for 代表，象征
What does "ESL" stand for?

stand back 退后，不介入
The paramedics told the crowd to **stand back**.

stand up 站起来
Alice **stood up** and ran across the field.

stare 盯着
staring, stared
His mother told him not to **stare** at him.

stay away 离开
Stay away from it. That animal is dangerous.

stay in 待在家里
I'll **stay in** and work.

stay out 待在外面
Peter wants to **stay out** late.

stay up 熬夜
You will go to school tomorrow. I don't want you to **stay up** late.

steal 偷
stealing, stole
He **stole** a cookie from the cookie jar.

steer 驾驶
steering, steered
She **steered** the ship through the strait.

stick out 伸出
The dog **stuck** its head **out** of the window.

stick together 互相支持
Families need to **stick together**.

stick up 竖起

The cat's ears **stick up**. 译

sting 叮，刺痛
stinging, stung

I got **stung** by a bee. 译

stink 发臭
stinking, stank

Fish begin to **stink** at the head. 译

stir 搅拌
stirring, stirred

Stir one cup of sugar into the batter. 译

stitch 缝补
stitching, stitched

He **stitched** a patch onto his coat. 译

stitch up 缝好

The doctor **stitched up** his wound. 译

stoop 弯腰
stooping, stooped

He had to **stoop** to pick it up. 译

stop up 堵塞

Something has **stopped up** the drain. 译

store 储存
storing, stored

Store the cookies in an airtight jar. 译

stretch 伸展
stretching, stretched

She **stretched** out in the bed. 译

string 串起来
stringing, strung

She **strung** the shells by a silver chain. 译

strike 撞击
striking, struck

The car **struck** the tree. 译

study 学习
studying, studied

Marie **studied** physics at university. 译

stuff 塞满
stuffing, stuffed

She **stuffed** the laundry bag full. 译

subtract 减去
subtracting, subtracted

If you **subtract** 10 from 23, you get 13. 译

succeed 成功
succeeding, succeeded

He **succeeded** in getting a place at an art school. 译

suck 吸
sucking, sucked

He **sucked** on his cigarette, although smoking is harmful to his health. 译

suit 适合
suiting, suited

Do white clothes **suit** me? 译

sun 晒太阳
sunning, sunned

It is better for you to **sun** yourself more. 译

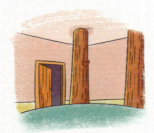

support 支撑
supporting, supported

The thick wooden posts **support** the ceiling. 译

surround 围绕,包围
surrounding, surrounded

A wall **surrounds** the old city. 译

swallow 吞咽
swallowing, swallowed

Chew your food well before you **swallow**. 译

sweat 出汗
sweating, sweated

He **sweats** a lot when he exercises. 译

sweep 打扫
sweeping, swept

Could you please **sweep** the floor? 译

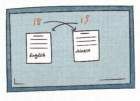

swell 肿胀，膨胀
swelling, swelled

Heavy rain **swelled** the river.

swim 游泳
swimming, swam

I can **swim** very fast.

switch 调换
switching, switched

The dates of the last two exams have been **switched**.

switch off 关上开关

He **switched** the TV **off**.

switch on 打开开关

She **switched** the light **on**.

Tt

take up 开始做……

He wants to **take up** swimming.

talk 讲话
talking, talked

Grandpa is not at home. You can **talk** to him in the morning.

tap 轻敲，轻拍
tapping, tapped

Someone was **tapping** on the door.

taste 品尝
tasting, tasted

Apple juice **tastes** good.

tear 撕破，流泪
tearing, tore

The bullet **tore** through his leg.

tear out 撕下

He **tore** a leaf **out** of his notebook.

tear up 毁坏

A batter is **tearing up** the league.

telephone 打电话
telephoning, telephoned

I am going to **telephone** my cousin tonight.

63

test 测试
testing, tested
I use flashcards to **test** myself. 译

thank 感谢
thanking, thanked
I **thanked** her for the present. 译

think of 发明，想出
I will **think of** something to wear for the fancy dress party. 译

thread 穿过，穿针线
threading, threaded
They **threaded** through the crowd. 译

throw away 扔掉
I should **throw away** that torn shirt. 译

tick 标出记号，打钩
ticking, ticked
Tick YES or NO to each question. 译

tick off 用记号标出，列出
Tick off your choice below. 译

tickle 发痒
tickling, tickled
My nose started to **tickle**. 译

tie 打结
tying, tied
I **tied** a knot in the rope. 译

tie up 束紧，捆绑
He **tied up** his shoelaces. 译

tighten 绷紧
tightening, tightened
The rope holding the boat suddenly **tightened** and broke. 译

tip 给小费
tipping, tipped
He **tipped** the servant in the restaurant. 译

64

tip over 翻倒
He accidentally **tipped** the lamp **over** and broke it.

tiptoe 踮起脚走
tiptoing, tiptoed
She **tiptoed** through the puddle.

toast 烘烤
toasting, toasted
Toast the bread lightly on both sides.

toss 扔
tossing, tossed
She **tossed** the paper into the recycling bin.

touch 触摸
touching, touched
Her tiny hands gently **touched** my face.

tour 旅行,旅游
touring, toured
We **toured** in London.

trace 追踪,描绘
tracing, traced
He **traced** the route on the map.

train 训练,培训
training, trained
I'm **trained** to be a volunteer for the Olympic Games.

trap 受困于……
trapping, trapped
He got **trapped** in the burning wreck.

travel 旅行
travelling, travelled
You'll **travel** around the world.

treat 对待
treating, treated
Don't **treat** me like a child.

tremble 颤抖
trembling, trembled
My voice **trembled** as I began to speak.

trick 戏弄
tricking, tricked

Kids says "**Trick** or treat!" at every house. 译

trip 绊倒
tripping, tripped

But suddenly he **tripped** and fell. 译

try on 试穿

Many girls **try on** the shoe, but it does not fit. 译

tuck 塞进
tucking, tucked

The letter had been **tucked** under a pile of papers. 译

turn 转弯
turning, turned

Turn right at the first crossing and the restaurant is on your left. 译

turn back 往回走

Soldiers barred the road so we had to **turn back**. 译

turn down 调小

Would you mind **turning down** the music? 译

turn off 关闭

It's so dark. Someone has **turned off** the light. 译

turn on 打开

Would you mind **turning on** the radio? 译

turn around 转过身

At the crossroads you **turn around** to face the road. 译

turn up 出现，露面

Hu Jin said she would meet him at the coffee shop but she didn't **turn up**. 译

twinkle 闪烁
twinkling, twinkled

Stars **twinkle** in the night sky. 译

twist 拧，扭曲
twisting, twisted

The girl **twisted** the toy into different shapes. 译

type 打字
typing, typed

I never learned how to **type**. 译

Uu

underline 在……下面画线，强调
underlining, underlined

His name was **underlined** in the book. 译

understand 明白
understanding, understood

I can **understand** what she's saying. 译

undress 脱衣服
undressing, undressed

She **undressed** and went to bed. 译

unfasten 解开
unfastening, unfastened

You may **unfasten** your seat belt now. 译

unload 卸下
unloading, unloaded

Could you help me **unload** the car? 译

unlock 解锁
unlocking, unlocked

How can I **unlock** my computer if I forget the password? 译

unpack 打开
unpacking, unpacked

He **unpacked** his bag. 译

unroll 铺开
unrolling, unrolled

I **unrolled** the new carpet. 译

untie 松开，解开
untying, untied

Can you **untie** this knot? 译

unwrap 打开
unwrapping, unwrapped

Don't **unwrap** your present until your birthday. 译

upset 打翻
upsetting, upset

I **upset** a cup of coffee onto my shirt. 译

urge 要求，催促
urging, urged

The rescuers **urged** us to remain calm. 译

use up 用完
Don't **use up** all the soap. Leave me some to wash with. 译

Vv

vacuum 用吸尘器清扫
vacuuming, vacuumed

Vacuum up the crumbs on the couch. 译

vanish 消失
vanishing, vanished

Many kinds of animals have **vanished** from the earth. 译

Ww

waddle 摇摇摆摆地走
waddling, waddled

A fat goose **waddled** across the yard. 译

wade 涉水
wading, waded

I jumped off the boat and **waded** back to the shore. 译

wag 摇动
wagging, wagged

The dog was **wagging** his tail. 译

wake up 醒来，叫醒

Dad **woke up** late for work this morning. 译

wander 漫步，徘徊
wandering, wandered

Grandpa was just **wandering** around the house. 译

68

warn 警告
warning, warned

The public sign **warns** us not to litter at random. 译

wash 洗
washing, washed

Do you often **wash** your clothes on the weekends? 译

wash up 洗漱，洗餐具

It will just take me a minute to **wash up** and then we can go. 译

watch 观看
watching, watched

They are **watching** TV. 译

watch out 小心，提防

Watch out! It could be dangerous. 译

watch over 看守

The shepherds **watched over** their sheep. 译

water 浇水
watering, watered

She is **watering** the flowers. 译

wave 挥手
waving, waved

We **waved** goodbye to each other. 译

wear out 穿破

We **wore out** the school uniforms. 译

weep 哭泣
weeping, wept

He **wept**. 译

weigh 称重
weighing, weighed

These bags usually **weigh** about 8~15 kilograms. 译

welcome 欢迎
welcoming, welcomed

We **welcome** you to our party. 译

wheel 变换方向，转动
wheeling, wheeled

He **wheeled** his motorcycle into the garage. 译

whip 搅拌，抽打
whipping, whipped

Whip the eggs, oils and honey together. 译

whisper 低声说，耳语
whispering, whispered

He **whispered** in my ear. 译

whistle 呼啸，吹口哨
whistling, whistled

We could hear the wind **whistling** through the trees. 译

wind 绕
winding, winded

The horse jumped forwards and rounded her, **winding** the rope round her waist. 译

wind up 给……上弦

Father **winds up** the clock once a week. 译

wink 眨眼
winking, winked

She **winked** and smiled at me. 译

wipe 擦
wiping, wiped

Would you **wipe** the dishes? 译

wonder 想知道，惊讶
wondering, wondered

I **wondered** what that noise was. 译

work out 算出

It **works out** cheaper to travel by bus. 译

worry 担心
worrying, worried

Don't **worry**. You'll be fine. 译

wound 受伤
wounding, wounded

Losing the match **wounded** his pride. 译

wrap 包
wrapping, wrapped

They were busy **wrapping** presents.

wriggle 蠕动，扭动
wriggling, wriggled

The baby is **wriggling** on his father's lap.

wring 拧
wringing, wrung

I **wrung** out my wet bathing suit.

wrinkle 弄皱
wrinkling, wrinkled

Try not to **wrinkle** your trousers.

write 写
writing, wrote

I'm writing an article about my father.

write down 记下
Please **write down** your answer on the answer sheet.

Yy

yawn 打哈欠
yawning, yawned

Students were **yawning** in class.

yell 喊叫
yelling, yelled

We saw people **yelling** for help.

Zz

zip 拉上拉链
zipping, zipped

I helped him **zip** his jacket.

zoom 疾驰而去
zooming, zoomed

They got in the car and **zoomed** away.

图书在版编目（CIP）数据

情景英语 4000 词 / 沧浪文化英语创研室编著. — 北京：北京大学出版社，2021.1
ISBN 978-7-301-31898-0

Ⅰ.①情… Ⅱ.①沧… Ⅲ.①英语–词汇–儿童教育–教学参考资料 Ⅳ.① H313

中国版本图书馆 CIP 数据核字 (2020) 第 248301 号

书　　　名	情景英语4000词 QINGJING YINGYU 4000 CI
著作责任者	沧浪文化英语创研室　编著
责 任 编 辑	刘文静　吴宇森
标 准 书 号	ISBN 978-7-301-31898-0
出 版 发 行	北京大学出版社
地　　　址	北京市海淀区成府路205号　100871
网　　　址	http://www.pup.cn　　新浪微博：@北京大学出版社
电 子 信 箱	wuyusen@pup.cn
电　　　话	邮购部 010-62752015　发行部 010-62750672 编辑部 010-62759634
印 刷 者	北京盛通印刷股份有限公司
经 销 者	新华书店 889毫米×1194毫米　16开本　18.5印张　150千字 2021年1月第1版　2021年1月第1次印刷
定　　　价	158.00元（全四册）

未经许可，不得以任何方式复制或抄袭本书之部分或全部内容。
版权所有，侵权必究
举报电话：010-62752024　电子信箱：fd@pup.pku.edu.cn
图书如有印装质量问题，请与出版部联系，电话：010-62756370